D1291133

A Senior's Guide to Healthy Travel

By
Donald L. Sullivan, R.Ph. M.S.

CAREER PRESS
180 Fifth Avenue
P.O. Box 34
Hawthorne, NJ 07507
1-800-CAREER-1
201-427-0229 (outside U.S.)
FAX: 201-427-2037

A SENIOR'S GUIDE TO HEALTHY TRAVEL
ISBN 1-56414-126-8, $14.95
Cover design by The Gottry Communications Group, Inc.
Printed in the U.S.A. by Book-mart Press

To order this title by mail, please include price as noted above, $2.50 handling per order, and $1.00 for each book ordered. Send to: Career Press, Inc., 180 Fifth Ave., P.O. Box 34, Hawthorne, NJ 07507

Or call toll-free 1-800-CAREER-1 (Canada: 201-427-0229) to order using VISA or MasterCard, or for further information on books from Career Press.

Library of Congress Cataloging-in-Publication Data

Sullivan, Donald, 1967-
    Senior's guide to healthy travel / by Donald Sullivan.
        p.   cm.
    Includes index.
    ISBN 1-56414-126-8 : $14.95
    1. Travel--Health aspects. 2. Aged--Travel. I. Title.
    RA783.5.S85   1994
    613.6'8'0846--dc20

                                                            94-27870
                                                            CIP

DEDICATION

To my parents, Jan and Donna Sullivan, my brother Jerry Sullivan, and a special loved one, Amy Newman, for all the love and support you gave me in writing this book.

Chapter 1

What you should know before you go

You've been planning this trip for a lifetime. And no doubt hoping it will be the first of many during your Golden Years. Whether you look forward to touring the world's great museums in style...roughing it in America's National Parks...soaking up the Caribbean sun on the deck of a cruise ship...or sampling the exotic cuisine of Southeast Asia...you probably aren't giving too much thought to blisters, bug bites, sunburn or (heaven forbid) diarrhea.

After all, any traveler has to cope with a few minor annoyances, right?

You're not any traveler. As a member of a new generation of seniors—healthier and more adventurous than ever before—you're likely to be traveling farther and for more extended periods than the average traveler.

The senior difference

Even if you've "never felt better," those physical and lifestyle changes that come with getting older can make even the healthiest senior more prone to conditions such as fatigue and heat stroke. Over the years, your skin has gotten thinner, so you're more susceptible to chapping and sunburn. Your heart and lungs have to work harder. You may be taking prescription medication that can complicate traveling abroad.

Am I trying to dampen your enthusiasm for travel? Quite the contrary! This book was compiled to give you a single (portable) resource with all the detailed information you need to know as a senior traveler...so you can enjoy healthy, stress-free travel for many years to come.

Won't common sense protect you?

Yes. Most of the time. You have the common sense to apply sunscreen regularly and not to drink the water in certain locales.

But did you know that some prescription drugs can increase your sensitivity to the sun? (I'll list them for you in Chapter 6.)

Or that trying a local remedy for a "common" case of traveler's diarrhea can be fatal? (You'll find safe remedies in Chapter 3.)

How to use this book

This book is designed to give you detailed information in a straight-forward format. Use it:

Before you finalize your reservations. Check out your medical insurance coverage and purchase additional traveler's health insurance, if necessary. This chapter will help you ask all the right questions. If you're still in the process of selecting a destination, check the index for specific references to destination(s) around the world.

As you're packing. The checklists in this chapter will help you remember everything. And when you're finished, don't forget to pack this book. It will make a valuable traveling companion.

While you're traveling. You'll find information at-a-glance, whenever you need help recognizing poison ivy (Chapter 11) or preventing motion sickness (Chapter 4) or treating a sunburn (Chapter 7). In the unlikely event of medical emergency en route, you'll find this book a reassuring resource. (See Chapter 12.)

Your Healthy Traveler's Kit

Three components should be an essential part of any Healthy Traveler's Kit:

♦ medicinal products/health aids

♦ emergency medical information form

♦ traveler's medical insurance information and forms

Medicinal products packing checklist

You may be tempted to lighten your load by leaving out something like antacid, for example. But imagine trying to find it at the corner drugstore in Timbuktu. The best remedy for most minor ailments you're likely to encounter while traveling is to carry these over-the-counter medicinal products and health aids with you. Here's a suggested packing list.

___ antacids
___ anti-diarrhea medicine
___ antihistamines
___ cough/cold products
___ hydrocortisone cream
___ aspirin or other mild pain reliever
___ motion-sickness medication
___ prescription medications
___ band-aids (first aid kit)
___ lip balm (with sunscreen)
___ sunscreens (in a range of appropriate SPFs)
___ insect repellent

A word about personal care products

Every individual has his or her own "can't do without it" list. My advice is to streamline your personal care routine as much as possible. Then compile a realistic checklist using the five-step strategy that follows.

Remember: Especially if you're traveling abroad, you'll want to pack a supply sufficient to cover your entire trip. (Do you really want to go through the frustration or embarrassment of explaining a product like Depends to a clerk who doesn't speak English?)

A 5-step packing strategy

1. **Make an inventory.** List everything in your medicine cabinet, vanity, dresser—or anywhere else you keep personal care items. Don't overlook small essentials, such as tweezers. Or items you need, but don't use regularly, such as Depends.

2. **Plan for every contingency.** Carefully review the itinerary you created. Will you be walking a lot more than usual? Throw in a tube of ointment for sore muscles.

3. **Consult fellow travelers.** Friends and/or family members who have traveled to the same or similar destinations can help you "remember" essential items. Ask what they wish they had thought to pack. Also contact your travel agent, tour company or resort for a standard packing list.

4. **Visit a travel specialties store.** You'll be thankful for space-saving collapsible hair dryers, travel-sized containers and other items designed to streamline your load.

5. **Check each item off**, after you place it in your suitcase.

Emergency medical information

This piece of paper could literally save your life if you should become incapacitated and unable to communicate with a doctor or local hospital personnel. Be sure to:

1. **Record accurate, up-to-date information.**

2. **Prepare multiple forms.** One for every member of your traveling party.

3. **Carry it with you.** Slip it inside your passport or wallet, so it is always accessible.

Are you sure you'll be insured while traveling?

Many health insurance carriers, such as Blue Cross/Blue Shield, cover medical care outside the U.S. But don't assume anything. Take the time to check the fine print. After all, you don't want any unpleasant surprises when you're far from home.

Emergency Medical Information Form

Name_____

Address_____

_____

_____

Telephone_____

Birth Date_____

Blood Type_____

Emergency Contact_____

_____

_____

Physician's Name_____

Physician's Phone_____

Dentist's Name_____

Dentist's Phone_____

Existing Medical Conditions_____

_____

_____

_____

Prescription Drugs You're Currently Taking_____

_____

_____

Drug Allergies_____

_____

Medical Insurance Name and Policy Number_____

_____

Other Important Information_____

_____

_____

At least three weeks before you depart...

1. **Read your health insurance policy.** Note what is—and is not—covered, especially while you're traveling outside the country.

   ♦ Some insurance companies, for example, require you to pay your bill upon your discharge from a foreign hospital. In some cases, you may have to pay a deposit before you can be admitted to a foreign hospital.

   ♦ Medicaid and Medicare benefits do not cover any medical treatment you receive outside the U.S., except in Mexico or Canada. That means that if you must be hospitalized in Europe, you will have to foot the entire bill.

   ♦ Most medical insurance will not cover the expense of evacuation to another hospital or the United States.

2. **Call your insurance representative.** Ask the following questions to confirm and clarify your coverage.

   ♦ Does my insurance cover medical treatment in the countries in which I will be traveling?

   ♦ Do I have to pay for medical treatment up front?

   ♦ When will I receive reimbursement from the insurance company?

   ♦ Does my insurance cover transportation to a medical facility or back to the U.S. for medical care?

   ♦ What information or claims forms does the medical facility overseas have to complete for me to receive reimbursement?

   ♦ What is my deductible for medical treatment that is performed overseas?

   ♦ Are pre-existing conditions covered under the travel health insurance policy?

   ♦ Are prescriptions purchased overseas covered?

   ♦ What about treatment not yet approved in the U.S.?

   ♦ Is emergency dental treatment covered?

3. **Find out how to file a claim.** Ask your insurance representative to walk you through the procedure for filing a claim to receive a speedy reimbursement.

4. **Ask for additional claim forms.** You'll have to present them to the attending physician or hospital personnel.

5. **Consider purchasing additional travel health insurance.** If your health insurance does not provide adequate coverage outside the United States, contact one of the following sources for more information about health insurance for travelers.

♦ The American Association of Retired People (AARP) offers travelers' coverage as part of its Medicare supplement packages.

♦ Most U.S. health insurance carriers offer inexpensive travel health insurance. Even if you don't use it (and let's hope you never do!), it's a good investment.

Your local travel agent also can provide you with the names of companies that provide health insurance for travelers. But beware. Some travel health insurance policies have hidden clauses that could cause some trouble down the road, when you can least afford it.

Next, let's take a look inside your traveling medicine cabinet.

IN SUMMARY...

☑ Use this book to prepare and pack for your trip—and as a portable resource while you're traveling.

☑ Prepare your Healthy Traveler's Kit containing a range of medicinal and health care products, such as antacids and anti-diarrhea medicine—especially if you'll be traveling outside the U.S.

☑ Complete and carry an emergency medical form that contains accurate and up-to-date medical information.

☑ Medicaid and Medicare do not cover medical treatment outside the U.S., except in Canada and Mexico.

☑ Review your medical insurance policy with an insurance representative to determine what will—and will not—be covered while you're traveling outside the country.

☑ Consult a travel agent, AARP or your insurance company for information about purchasing additional traveler's health insurance.

☑ Preparation is your passport to healthy, crisis-free travel. When you've taken precaution to cover every contingency, you're free to really relax and enjoy your trip.

Chapter 2

Your traveling medicine cabinet

If prescription medications are part of your daily life at home, they will be an equally important part of your life on the road.

Most prescription medications can be refilled at any pharmacy throughout the U.S. But traveling abroad can present a few problems. You'll need to be armed with these strategies for coping with "medication lag," sidestepping tangles with customs officials and quickly replacing any prescription medications that may be lost or stolen.

Pre-trip precautions

Ask about immunizations. Your physician will be able to give you the most up-to-date information.

Purchase more medication than you'll need. An extra week's supply is a good rule of thumb.

Ask your doctor for duplicate prescriptions. Use these typed prescriptions—containing both generic and brand names—as a backup in case your medication is lost or stolen.

Subscribe to Medic Alert if you have chronic health problems or drug allergies. This 24-hour-a-day service will provide vital information about your health to a physician calling from anywhere in the world. If you are unconscious or unable to communicate in an emergency situation, this could save your life. For more information, call (800) ID ALERT.

A painless plan for traveling with medication

1. **Carry all prescription medications with you.** You'll avoid potential problems with customs officials by carrying all medication in their original bottles. Never pack medications in your suitcase. Your luggage may be lost.

2. **Carry a letter from your doctor.** Some countries are reluctant to allow entry to anyone traveling with prescribed sedatives, tranquilizers and other narcotics. In addition to your duplicate (typed) prescriptions, present a letter signed by your physician that states why you need the drug or drugs in question.

3. **Don't purchase medications in other countries.** Many medications that are available only by prescription in the United States are readily available without a prescription overseas. Stick to your own prescription. In some cases, these drugs do not have FDA approval, so you can't be sure they are safe for you. And you may run into problems at U.S. customs if you try to bring them back into this country.

4. **Avoid "medication lag."** Whenever you travel across one or more time zones to reach your destination, the effects of your medication may "lag." Just as your body clock must adjust to jet lag, you will have to adjust your medication dosing schedule to match the time zone in your destination.

   If you're crossing several time zones, try to stay on the same dosing schedule you use at home. For example, say you are accustomed to taking your medication at 8 a.m. everyday at home in New York. Once you arrive in London,—where the time is five hours later than in New York—your "8 a.m." medication should be taken five hours later, or 1 p.m. London time.

   Tip: If you're afraid you'll get confused or have to track several medications, it may help to keep an inexpensive wristwatch set on home time.

5. **Use a dessicator in hot, humid climates.** Available free at any pharmacy, a dessicator placed in each bottle will prevent moisture from reducing the effectiveness of your prescription medications.

"Over-the-counter" in other countries

As I've told you, many drugs available by prescription here are sold over the counter in other countries. Mexico is an prime example.

Walk into any Mexican pharmacy and you can purchase most of your prescription drugs over-the-counter—often for half of what you would pay in the states.

This has tempted many Americans to "stock up" on otherwise costly prescription drugs during trips south of the border. In fact, some travelers claim to save enough on drugs to more than pay for their entire trip!

How can Mexico and other countries sell brand-name medications so cheap? There are two possible explanations.

♦ **National health insurance.** When the government is the number-one drug consumer, it has the clout to dictate prices to drug manufacturers.

♦ **Governmental price controls.** In some cases, these controls limit the profits a drug manufacturer can take. In others, they keep a lid on the prices of specific drugs.

Over-the-counter can leave you out-of-pocket

The FDA has documented numerous cases in which medicinal products purchased over-the-counter in foreign countries actually contained no drug at all. Here's how the "scam" has worked in the past.

At one time, it was common practice for an overseas firm to buy a drug manufactured by a U.S. company, empty the capsules of medicinal powder and fill them with talc or lactose. The medicinal powder was then imported back into the U.S. for sale—while the phony capsules were put up for sale in the offending country!

Of course, laws now prohibit this practice, but illegal importers and exporters within some developing countries continue to practice this scam. Even if foreign capsules look exactly like the capsules you purchase at your local pharmacy, you can never be sure that they contain the medicine they claim.

The other danger is, you may be buying outdated or expired drugs. When a drug passes its expiration date, 10 percent of its active ingredients have disintegrated. The older it gets, the less potent it becomes. In some cases, drugs become poisonous substances as they disintegrate.

Tips for safe shopping

The risks associated with buying prescription drugs in other countries nearly always outweigh the money to be saved. Here are a few important tips for safe shopping.

Stick with the brand names you know. If you must buy medications in a foreign country, stick to brand names you know. Never buy generics.

Purchase sealed or tamper-proof bottles or packages.

Consult a qualified local doctor or pharmacist. If you have any questions take the time to get professional advice.

Never buy products manufactured in developing countries. Most of these locally manufactured products aren't subject to the strict quality control regulations in place in the U.S.

Always check the expiration date. If you can't find it on the bottle, it has probably been removed with acetone, so don't buy it.

The lowdown on local remedies

Say you return after a day of sightseeing with a throbbing headache. Or, despite your care, you wake up with a case of traveler's diarrhea. It's not the end of the world. Unless you turn to a local remedy.

No matter what your distress, never accept a local remedy. Some remedies are combinations of useless ingredients. For example, a burn remedy confiscated in Mexico was found to contain sawdust, coffee and dirt. But in far too many instances, travelers have been seriously harmed by local remedies.

Here are a few more chilling examples of some local remedies purported to cure traveler's diarrhea:

♦ Iodochlorhydroxyquin (more commonly known as Mexaform) can cause serious damage to the central nervous system.

♦ Greta or Azarcon contains high amounts of lead and has been known to be fatal.

♦ Gordolobo yerba herbal tea can result in serious liver damage.

After a few reports like these, it shouldn't be hard to remember to pack your own anti-diarrhea medication before you leave home.

Now it's time to take off. If you're flying, turn to the next chapter for tips on how to relieve jet lag. If you're traveling by cruise ship, train or car, it's motion sickness you'll be most concerned with. Skip ahead to Chapter 4.

IN SUMMARY...

☑ Carry more medication than you'll need during your trip. An extra week's supply is a good rule of thumb.

☑ Always carry duplicate—and typed—prescriptions containing both generic and brand names as a backup in case your medication is lost or stolen.

☑ If you have chronic health problems or drug allergies, subscribe to Medic Alert. Call (800) ID ALERT for more information.

☑ Always carry prescription medications with you—in their original bottles.

☑ If you're traveling with prescription sedatives, tranquilizers or other narcotics, carry a letter signed by your doctor stating why you need the drugs.

☑ Do not purchase prescription medications over the counter in another country, especially in developing countries.

☑ Avoid "medication lag" by staying on the same dosing schedule you use at home.

☑ Use a dessicator in each prescription bottle to prevent moisture from reducing the effectiveness of your prescription medication in hot, humid climates.

☑ If you must purchase prescription or over-the-counter drugs in a foreign country, purchase sealed or tamper-proof bottles or packages with a clearly marked expiration date.

☑ Avoid local remedies—which range from useless to dangerous.

Chapter 3

Catching up
with jet lag

Unless you plan to embark on a leisurely cruise, travel by train or car to your destination, you are probably looking forward to putting the miles between your home and your destination behind you in as short a time as possible. These days, it's common to fly across the country— or nearly halfway across the world— before the sun sets on the first day of your trip.

The only problem is that the more time zones your body crosses, the further behind your body clock lags. The result is a "disease" commonly known to all of us as jet lag.

Jet lag is really nothing more than a confused body clock. When your flight touches down in a time zone in which the sun rises and sets several hours ahead of your body's normal schedule, your physiological processes are out of synch. Until your body clock resets itself, you're likely to be wide-eyed at 3 a.m. and ravenous at 3 in the afternoon. Other common symptoms of jet lag

are dizziness, headaches and sore muscles.

Is there any way to beat jet lag?

Opt for a slower mode of travel. Taking the train or a cruise will give your body a chance to adjust to each different time zone. (And you'll enjoy the view.) Another way to beat jet lag is to travel within the same time zone, directly north or south, for example.

Here are several factors that influence how severe the effects of jet lag will be and how long you're likely to feel it.

The direction you travel. Traveling east produces more severe jet lag than traveling west. Here's why: Say you leave for the east coast at 8 a.m. pacific coast time. By the time the clock tells you it's time to turn in, 11 p.m. that night, your body clock insists it's still only 8 p.m. Too early to go to bed! But when the wake-up call comes at 7 a.m. the next morning, your body clock may be in a deep 4 a.m. slumber. The farther you travel, the more dramatic the effect.

But say you leave New York at 5 p.m. and arrive in San Francisco at 9 p.m. (midnight in New York). By the time you collect your bags and settle in, you're ready to turn in at 11 p.m. After all, your body tells you it's 2 a.m!

The number of time zones you cross. Cross one time zone and the effects are fairly minimal. But each new time zone multiplies the symptoms of jet lag.

Stress. Pre-trip anxiety, the last-minute dash to your gate and other sources of stress only compound the effects of jet lag.

The quality of your trip. Many factors during your flight prey on your body's defenses against jet lag: low humidity, excessive noise and vibration, turbulence, sitting for long periods, and a warm, stuffy atmosphere are also factors.

How much you drink. Double the effects of every cocktail you have inflight. If you drink or eat more than you normally would before, during or after your flight, you're asking for discomfort.

How much caffeine you consume. The caffeine in coffee or soft drinks may ward off fatigue temporarily, but in the end this will only intensify the effects of jet lag.

Starting out right

1. **Time your flight according to the direction you're traveling.** When you're traveling east, book an early flight. When you're traveling west, book an afternoon or evening flight. This timing will most closely match your natural schedule, so it will be easier for your body to adjust to a new time zone.

2. **Adjust your schedule before you leave.** This can be done very simply. Beginning three days before your trip, go to bed earlier and get up earlier if you're traveling east and later, if you're traveling west. When you arrive, try to socialize a bit before turning in for the night. This will also help your body adjust to the new environment.

3. **Try a jet lag diet.** Do jet lag diets really work? Some frequent travelers swear by them. Others report they are not only inconvenient, but ultimately worthless. If you feel it's worth a try, consult your physician first. Then, begin three days before you leave on your next trip.

   ♦ **Day one:** "Feast" on a high-protein breakfast and lunch, and a high carbohydrate dinner.

   ♦ **Day two:** Fast, eating smaller, low-calorie, low

carbohydrate meals, such as fruits, vegetables and salads.

♦ **Day three:** Feast again.

♦ **Departure day:** Fast.

♦ **When you arrive:** Break your fast with a high-protein meal.

Many health food stores sell special "anti-jet lag" vitamin and amino acid products. There is no clinical evidence that supports their effectiveness, so don't waste your money.

How to help your body clock "catch up" en route

The good news is that there are many things you can do to prevent—or at least minimize—the effects of jet lag.

Drink plenty of fluids. Water and fruit juice will help your body compensate for the dry atmosphere in the airplane cabin.

Eat light meals. Overeating puts extra stress on your body, even in the best of circumstances. Choose fruits, vegetables, chicken and pasta over steak and heavy sauces.

Wear loose-fitting clothing. Comfort is the key to reducing stress, especially when you're confined to a small space for several hours or more.

Avoid caffeine and alcohol. Their effects will be intensified by the altitude and cabin atmosphere. It may be tempting to use coffee or cocktails to wake up or sedate yourself, but in the end they will only dehydrate your body. Stay with water and fruit juices and "virgin" cocktails—at least until you've reached your final destination.

Exercise. That's right. You can do simple isometric exercises (contracting different muscle groups for shorts periods of time) even in your cramped coach seat on the airplane. Every hour or so, step into the aisle to stretch and take a short walk.

Keep your "home" schedule while traveling. If you're only a time zone or two away, it may be easier on your body to eat a few hours later or turn in earlier.

What other remedies are available?

Many travelers have had success with "light therapy," because light plays such an important part in regulating our body clocks. Here's how it works.

If you're traveling east, crossing up to six time zones: Get out in the bright sunlight during the morning on the first few days after you arrive. You can substitute bathroom light if the weather is cold or cloudy.

If you're traveling west, up to six time zones: Expose yourself to bright light at the end of each day.

If you are crossing more than six time zones in either direction: Avoid bright light until midday.

If you decided to book a cruise, rather than a transcontinental flight, you may trade jet lag for another problem. In the next chapter, we'll explore the ups and downs of motion sickness.

IN SUMMARY...

☑ You can beat jet lag by opting for a slower mode of travel, such as a cruise, or traveling directly north or south, as long as you travel in the same time zone.

☑ Traveling east results in more severe jet lag than traveling west. Try to book an early flight when traveling east and an afternoon or evening flight when you're traveling west.

☑ Every time zone you cross multiplies the symptoms of jet lag.

☑ Stress, alcohol, caffeine, dry air, excessive noise and vibration, turbulence and sitting for long periods all compound the effects of jet lag.

☑ Eat light meals and drink plenty of fluids before and during your flight. Jet lag diets work for some travelers.

☑ Wear loose-fitting clothes. Do isometric exercises in your seat and stretch your legs by walking up and down the aisle of the airplane every hour or so.

Chapter 4

The ups and downs of motion sickness

If you're part of an estimated one-third of the population prone to motion sickness, you may be a bit queasy about planning even a short cruise. Before you decide to live out your life as a confirmed landlubber, you should know that there are many ways to prevent— or at least substantially diminish— the symptoms of motion sickness.

You may think you're immune to motion sickness if you have never experienced it, but you should know it can strike without warning, even if you're traveling by airplane or car.

The first sign of motion sickness will be clearly visible to your companions. Your complexion will suddenly appear pale. You may then appear flushed and feel restless, perhaps yawn a lot. Next, you'll break into a cold sweat. Your hands will feel cold and clammy and your underarms will become drenched with perspiration. Your mouth will be dry and your stomach queasy. If you become queasy enough, you may vomit.

Left untreated, motion sickness will usually disappear in one to three days, as your body adjusts to your new environment. That's not too reassuring when you're flat on your back in your cabin for half of your trip.

To keep motion sickness from grounding you, be prepared.

How to prevent it

Hold your head still. Brace your head against the back of your chair. Or lay in a semi-reclined position, keeping your head as still as possible.

Focus on the horizon. Or pick out any distant object and concentrate only on it.

Avoid spicy foods. Rich or spicy foods may be hard to digest, adding to your queasiness. If you're on a cruise, choose from the abundance of fresh fruits and breads served on shipboard buffets.

At the first sign of queasiness, stop eating. Try not to eat or drink anything for four to six hours. If you become dehydrated, drink only small amounts of flat cola, ginger ale or Gatorade. When you feel up to eating, slowly add foods that are easy to digest—such as bananas, rice, breads, gelatin and applesauce.

Avoid overindulging. Eat a light meal and don't drink alcohol the night before you depart.

Get lots of fresh air. It may be tempting to retire to your cabin below board, but you'll feel more comfortable breathing fresh air in your deck chair. If you're traveling by plane, open the air vents.

Avoid reading. The contrast of the small type and the movement in your peripheral vision will make you feel worse.

Select a mid-ship cabin. If you know you're prone to motion sickness, choose a cabin as close to the waterline as possible. On a plane, chose a center seat, over the wing.

Drive, rather than ride. If you can't drive, sit in the front seat. If you're traveling by train, face forward and sit near the window.

Drugs that prevent or treat motion sickness

Which drugs prevent or treat motion sickness? There are a number of drugs available over-the-counter, and a prescription drug called Transderm Scop Patch. Always consult your doctor or pharmacist before making a choice.

Over-the-counter antihistamines. Dramamine, Bonine, Triptone and Benadryl are all safe and effective when taken one or two hours before you depart. A common side effect of these medications is drowsiness. You may also experience dry mouth, blurred vision and/or constipation.

Bonine has an advantage over the others. It is taken once daily and may make you less drowsy.

Caution: Be sure to read the warning statements on the side of the package before using any of these products. If you have asthma, glaucoma, obstructive diseases of the gastrointestinal or urinary tract, emphysema or other chronic lung disease, or prostate problems, consult your doctor or pharmacist before using these products.

If you drink alcohol or take other prescription medications, such as tranquilizers, with these drugs, drowsiness becomes severe.

Meclizine (brand names: Bonine and Drama-mine II) may be your best choice. Take it at least an hour before you depart, then again every 24 hours. The key advantage of this drug is that it won't make you as drowsy as other motion sickness drugs.

Cyclizine (brand name: Marezine) should be taken half an hour before you depart, and then every four to six hours afterward.

Dimenhydrinate (brand names: Dramamine, Triptone, Calm-X) should be taken an hour before departure to prevent motion sickness. Failing that, you can use it to stop the symptoms of motion sickness by taking it every four to six hours. One drawback is that it will make you drowsier than any other motion sickness medication.

Phosphorated Carbohydrate (brand names: Emetrol, Especol) is formulated to help you stop vomiting. Take one to two tablespoonsful in 15-minute intervals until the vomiting stops. Doses should be limited to five per hour. If vomiting doesn't stop after five doses, contact a doctor.

Caution: This product contains high concentrations of glucose and should not be used by diabetics. Read the directions carefully.

What about patches?

Adhesive patches, such as the *Transderm Scop Patch*, contain the clinically tested prescription medication scopolamine that prevents motion sickness, nausea and vomiting for up to three days.

Four hours before you depart, place one patch (about the size of a nickel) on skin that is clean and free of hair or abrasions behind one of your ears. The drug is slowly administered through your skin.

If your trip lasts longer than three days, or if the patch falls off, place a fresh patch behind your other ear. One box contains four patches, enough for two people on a week-long cruise.

Be sure to wash your hands thoroughly immediately after applying the patch. If some of the drug remains on your hands and you happen to rub your eyes, your vision can become blurred temporarily.

About two in three people experience dry mouth when using the patch. Drink plenty of fluids or suck on hard candy. Drowsiness also occurs in about one in six patch users, but it may be less severe than the drowsiness caused by other motion sickness medications such as Dramamine.

Caution: Drinking alcohol while using the patch may increase drowsiness. Take care if you're driving.

Again, if you have: glaucoma; metabolic, liver or kidney disease; obstructions of the stomach, bladder, or intestines; difficulty urinating, or are taking other prescription medications, consult your doctor and/or pharmacist.

Congratulations! You've arrived safe and sound—and feeling fine. But if you're traveling to one of the many destinations worldwide where it's not advisable to drink the water, you'll have to remain vigilant. Or you may encounter another unpleasant "companion"...traveler's diarrhea. We will tackle that subject in Chapter 5.

IN SUMMARY...

☑ Left untreated, motion sickness will usually disappear in one to three days, as your body adjusts to your new environment.

☑ You can prevent motion sickness by keeping your head motionless and focusing on a distant object or the horizon.

☑ Avoid too much spicy food or alcohol, beginning the night before you depart on your trip.

☑ Get plenty of fresh air. Stay above board on a ship, and open up your air vent on an airplane.

☑ Avoid reading. The contrast of the small type and the movement in your peripheral vision will make you feel worse.

☑ Select a cabin as close to the waterline as possible or a seat over the wing on an airplane. If you're traveling by car, drive or sit in the front passenger seat. If you're traveling by train, face forward and sit near the window.

Chapter 5

Dodging traveler's diarrhea

Traveling to Central or South America, Africa, the Middle East, Southeast Asia or the Caribbean? Along with the exotic sights, sounds and foods, you may take in something you haven't bargained for. One innocent bite of lettuce or a slightly undercooked piece of fish can lay you up with stomach cramps, fever, chills, vomiting—and a nasty case of traveler's diarrhea.

It happens to the best of travelers. An estimated 40 to 50 percent—even those taking the best precautions—fall victim to this ailment while visiting developing countries.

Traveler's diarrhea is caused by infectious bacteria in water and uncooked foods. It can strike even in places where sanitation seems to be very good. In fact, even subtle changes in the water throughout the U.S. can affect domestic travelers. However, the symptoms are far less severe.

Prevention is the best treatment. The odds are in your favor if you stay away from foods considered "risky." Although it may take some getting used to, make a habit of being scrupulous about everything you put in your mouth while visiting high-risk countries.

The eight offenders

Memorize this list of foods and beverages and check it against every meal or snack—even if you're dining in the fanciest hotel.

1. leafy green vegetables

2. custards, pastries and other desserts

3. raw vegetables and cold platters

4. raw shellfish

5. raw meat, such as steak tartare

6. any undercooked seafood or meat

7. raw eggs, fresh cheeses or milk

8. tap water and ice cubes made from tap water

Be especially wary of:

♦ food sold by street vendors, unless you have seen it boiled

♦ hot sauces that have been sitting out on a restaurant table

♦ buffet-style foods that are not steaming hot

♦ brushing your teeth with tap water (use bottled water instead.)

Does this mean you have to live in constant fear or self- denial? Not when you stick to the following "safe" foods and beverages.

What foods are safe?

High temperatures will kill dangerous bacteria, so you're safe selecting any food or menu item that is baked, boiled or steamed. Accustom yourself to drinking only canned and bottled water and beverages such as soft drinks and beer.

Here's a brief rundown:

♦ anything boiling or steaming hot

♦ bottled water, beer or soft drinks

♦ bread and tortillas

♦ packaged butter or jelly

♦ any fresh fruit, vegetable or nut you have to peel or shell to eat

♦ undiluted fruit juices

♦ well done meat or seafood dishes, eaten while they are hot

♦ cooked eggs

♦ pasteurized and refrigerated dairy products

♦ coffee and hot tea

When is it okay to drink the water?

Although most major cities around the world have treated water systems and many modern hotels have installed efficient water purification systems, this may not be the case in developing countries. Here are five steps to ensure protection in even the most elegant hotel.

Ask. The personnel at your hotel should be able to tell you whether the tap water is treated or cleaned through a purification system. If you have any reason to suspect that the water is contaminated, use the following precautions.

Drink only hot beverages. Coffee and tea and bottled beverages (beer, wine and carbonated soft drinks, for example) are safe to drink anytime. Never drink anything served over ice. This "slip" catches up with more travelers than any other.

Wipe off your eating utensils before you eat. They may have been washed with contaminated water.

Don't brush your teeth with tap water. Use a carbonated beverage or bottled or boiled water.

Purify your own water. Here are four methods.

♦ **Boil it** for at least 10 minutes. It is important to rinse glassware in boiling water because purified water can easily be recontaminated when you place it in dirty glassware.

Add iodine. A concentration of 2 percent tincture of iodine (available at your local pharmacy) will purify contaminated tap water. If the water is clear, add five drops of the iodine to each quart. And if the water is cloudy, add 10 drops to the same quantity of water. Let the iodine-treated water stand for 30 minutes before using.

Caution: If you have a thyroid problem or are allergic to iodine, choose another method of purification.

♦ **Add Potable-Aqua tablets.** Campers and hikers commonly use this product to purify water from ponds and streams. Dissolve one tablet in a liter of water and wait at least 15 minutes before drinking water at room temperature, and 30 minutes for cool water.

♦ **Filter water through a coffee filter.** Use this method only if none of the others are available. It is not the most effective treatment, but it is better than nothing.

What's the best way to treat traveler's diarrhea?

Let's say that, despite your best efforts, you begin to feel the symptoms of a bout of traveler's diarrhea three to seven days after you arrive. Your first move? Go directly to your Healthy Traveler's Kit for some of the following portable treatments.

Imodium-AD. According to many doctors and pharmacists, this may be your best choice for treating acute diarrhea. When used as directed, it usually stops diarrhea and helps relieve the accompanying stomach cramps after only one dose.

Kaopectate, Diasorb, Donnagel. These drugs control diarrhea by absorbing excess water in the gastrointestinal tract. They offer safe and effective relief, typically after more than one dose.

Pepto-Bismol. There is some evidence that the large amounts of bismuth subsalicylate (a derivative of aspirin) in Pepto-Bismol may be effective in preventing traveler's diarrhea. However, you will have to chew two tablets four times every day—the equivalent of 8.3 aspirin tablets—for the first two weeks you are traveling to get this benefit.

Caution: Choose this option with care. The National Institute of Health concluded in 1985 that the benefit of using Pepto-Bismol to prevent traveler's diarrhea does not justify the risk, especially if: you're sensitive or allergic to aspirin; suffer from bleeding disorders; gout; or already take prescription drugs containing aspirin compounds, such as probenecid, methotrexate or coumadin.

Prescription antibiotics

Doxycycline and **Bactrim DS**. These two antibiotics are commonly prescribed to prevent traveler's diarrhea. Treatment usually begins on the first day of travel and continues until the second day after your return home.

Caution: These drugs should be restricted to travelers visiting high-risk areas on critical business or anyone with a serious health condition or underlying health problem that would make them more susceptible to diarrhea. Extensive consultation with a physician should occur before choosing this option.

Treating dehydration

Dehydration often occurs as a result of the diarrhea. Replace lost water and electrolytes by alternately drinking the following two liquids.

1. A glass of fruit juice (such as apple, orange or grapefruit) with a half-teaspoon of honey and a pinch of salt.

2. Any carbonated soft drink with one-fourth teaspoon of baking soda.

Caution: If diarrhea persists for more than four days, severe cramping occurs, your stomach feels tender or you notice bloody stools, stop all treatment and see a doctor immediately.

What about local remedies? Never use them. Drugs such as Entero-Vioform and Mexaform are not only ineffective, but toxic.

While you're getting accustomed to the differences in a tropical locale, don't forget that the sun—something you're very familiar with—can be even more potent close to the equator. Before you overdo it, take a few minutes to brush up on safe tanning in the next chapter.

IN SUMMARY...

☑ Remember, traveler's diarrhea is a result of what you eat and drink rather than where you're traveling.

☑ Although the bacteria that causes traveler's diarrhea is most often found where food is prepared under poor sanitary conditions, even elegant restaurants can be culprits.

☑ Always wipe off your eating utensils before you eat.

☑ Be sure to brush your teeth with boiled, bottled or purified water.

☑ Always carry an anti-diarrhea medication, such as Imodium-AD to treat traveler's diarrhea. Consult your doctor or pharmacist before choosing an over-the-counter or prescription medication.

☑ Memorize the "eight offenders," risky foods you should avoid at all costs.

☑ Never use a local remedy to treat a case of traveler's diarrhea.

Chapter 6

Staying on the sunny side of suntanning

More leisure time during your Golden Years often means more time spent outdoors year-round. Whether you're traveling or at home, a golden tan often seems to come with the territory.

For most of us, a suntan has become a symbol of health and beauty. What self-respecting vacationer of any age would return without an enviable suntan?

The A's and B's of tanning

The moment you step into the sunlight, your skin begins to react to the sun's ultraviolet (UV) rays by producing melanin, the brown pigment we call a suntan. Like a natural "armor," this pigment protects the skin's surface, as well as many underlying layers of tissue, from damage.

Sunlight is made up of two kinds of ultraviolet (UV) light.

UV-A, or "tanning" rays. These are thought to be relatively benign rays. They are present all year long. These are the only type of rays you'll bask in if you frequent a tanning booth because our skin can absorb more of them without burning. (We'll talk more about the pros and cons of this method of tanning later in this chapter.) But exposure over an extended period may still cause premature aging and skin cancer.

UV-B, or "burning" rays. A thousand times more potent than UV-A rays, these rays are most intense in the summertime and at midday (between the hours of 11 a.m. and 3 p.m.).

Three "shades" of tan

Not every tan is created equal. There are three distinct ways to get a suntan.

The sunburn tan. If you've ever tried to "rush" a tan—hitting the beach at midday on your first day in the tropics—you may know the first stage of a tan as sunburn. Many times, sunburn darkens into a tan within 24 hours of exposure. This "quick" tan occurs after three to seven days of exposure and is a result of the melanin in your skin oxidizing. This type of tan usually fades quickly—within two to four days—and then peels four to seven days after that.

The short-term tan. This type of "quick" tan is the result of an increase in the dispersion and oxidation of melanin. Stay out of the sun for a few days and your tan will fade almost as quickly as it appeared.

The long-term tan. This is the healthiest way to tan. With regular exposure to direct sunlight, your body gradually builds pigmentation that results in a "deep" tan. This type of tan peaks over a period of about two weeks. It will fade gradually, unless you continue to spend time in the sun.

Protect yourself: choose the right sunscreen

With each passing year, your skin becomes more and more susceptible to damage caused by the sun's burning rays. Wearing a sunscreen with the proper level of protection for your skin type is essential. It's also wise to limit your exposure to the sun, especially during 11 a.m. and 3 p.m.

1. **Choose the right type.** There are two basic types of sunscreen: Physical sunscreens, such as zinc oxide and titanium oxide, are products that reflect up to 99 percent of the sun's rays away from hard-to-protect areas, such as your cheeks, nose, lips and ears. Chemical sunscreens absorb the sun's rays so they cannot reach your skin. But make sure you check the label. The chemicals used differ by sunscreen—and all are not equally effective.

- **PABA (para-amino-benzoic-acid), padimate O,** or **padimate.** These chemicals, found in products such as Sundown, PreSun, Photoplex, Bain de Soleil and Hawaiian Tropic (sunscreen), are formulated to stay on your skin longer.

- **Benzophenones, cinnamates or salicylate derivatives.** These chemicals, used in Hawaiian Tropic tanning products and most Coppertone and Shade products, don't bind to your skin as well as the products mentioned above. This means you'll have to reapply them more frequently.

- **Photoplex.** This product effectively blocks UV-A rays, and UV-B ("burning" rays).

2. Choose the right level of protection. Once you've chosen the type of sunscreen you like, it's time to think about the level of protection

it offers. This is measured by the skin protection factor, or SPF.

The number of the SPF rating is the number of times the sunscreen will multiply your own skin's natural protection in the sun. For example, if your skin usually begins to burn after 15 minutes in direct sunlight, an SPF of 10 will protect you from UV-B or "burning" rays 10 times longer—150 minutes or two and a half hours.

Even if you are very fair, it doesn't pay to invest in SPF protection above 30. In fact, the FDA reports that sunscreens above SPF 30 provide only a minimal amount of extra protection. SPF 30 blocks 96.6 percent of the sun's burning rays. SPF 50 blocks 98 percent, only 1.4 percent more. Save your money. First, determine your skin type. Everyone's skin has a different degree of natural protection against the sun's burning rays. If you have olive skin, dark hair and brown eyes, you're likely to have more melanocytes that produce more protective melanin than a blue-eyed blond will. Use the following scale to determine your "skin protection factor."

♦ **Type 1:** You have very fair skin and red or blond hair. You may even have freckles. You never tan; you just burn—after only seven minutes in direct sunlight. **Recommended SPF: 20-30**

♦ **Type 2:** You have fair skin, so you burn very easily—after only 15 minutes in the sun. When you do tan, it is very light. **Recommended SPF: 12-20**

♦ **Type 3:** You eventually do tan. But you have to be very careful, because your skin can begin to burn after only 21 minutes in the sun. **Recommended SPF: 10-15**

♦ **Type 4:** Your skin has a medium tone, so you always tan and rarely ever burn. Still, your unprotected skin can begin to burn after only 28 minutes in the sun. **Recommended SPF: 6-10**

♦ **Type 5:** Your skin tone is medium to dark, so you seldom, if ever, burn. **Recommended SPF: 4-6**

♦ **Type 6:** Your skin is very dark or black so you never burn. You tan darkly. **Recommended: SPF 2-4.**

3. **Use sunscreen properly.** Even if you've been using sunscreen regularly for years, take a moment to review the following tips.

♦ **Use sunscreen even on overcast days.** When it's

cloudy, 80 percent of the sun's burning rays will still reach your skin. Even if you think you're safe under an umbrella, the sun's rays can reach you by reflecting off nearby water or sand.

♦ **Shake the bottle.** Be sure you shake it well, before applying the sunscreen to your skin.

♦ **Be generous.** Apply a generous amount of sunscreen to dry skin 15 to 30 minutes before you go outside. Most people don't apply enough sunscreen. Use about one ounce to cover your entire body. Too little will give you a false sense of security.

♦ **Rub it in.** Then allow 10 to 15 minutes for your skin to absorb it before you get dressed or apply makeup.

♦ **Reapply sunscreen every hour or two.** (more often if you are swimming or sweating).

Other sun-protection hints

Cover up. If a sunscreen provides three hours of protection, protect yourself from overexposure by covering up or going indoors after your time is up. But beware. If your T-shirt or beach robe is wet, 20 to 30 percent of the sun's burning rays may still reach your skin.

Choose waterproof sunscreen. If you plan to spend a lot of time in the water—where 90 percent of the sun's burning rays can still reach you—waterproof sunscreen will stay on your skin longer than water-resistant sunscreen and twice as long as regular sunscreen (up to 80 minutes). Sunscreens that are sweat-resistant will stay on your skin for up to 30 minutes even when you're perspiring heavily.

Stop using a sunscreen if you develop an allergic reaction. If your skin begins to itch, burn, sting or you develop a rash, ask your doctor or pharmacist to recommend another sunscreen.

Consult your doctor. If you are taking medication, your skin may be more sensitive to the sun. See a list of medications that may cause sun sensitivity on pages 44 and 45. Your doctor or pharmacist can recommend a level of protection.

Don't forget to protect your lips. Unlike the rest of the skin on your body, your lips can't tan. But they can burn. Wiping, licking, biting and picking at damaged skin only causes further damage. You will find many pleasant-tasting lip balms that protect lips, yet stay put.

Not all chapsticks have sunscreen, so when you're shopping for lip protection, look for these key words: "sunblock," "lip protector," or an SPF. PreSun 15 Lip Protector and Chapstick Sunblock are two effective choices. Make sure you purchase a product with an SPF of at least 15 to provide maximum protection.

Apply sunscreen to your lips 45 minutes to an hour before sun exposure and reapply every hour and before and after swimming, eating or drinking. If you notice redness or inflammation, stop using the product immediately.

Sunglasses: the eyes have it

Excessive exposure to the sun's ultraviolet (UV) rays may also cause permanent damage to the retina or cornea. A good pair of sunglasses should be an essential part of your traveling gear.

But before you reach for those fashion frames on sale at the local drug store, you should know that price usually has little to do with effectiveness. In fact, you may pay a higher price for a pair of designer shades and still have to squint through a day at the beach.

How do you choose the right sunglasses? First, make sure they provide UV protection. Most sunglasses fall into three basic categories, offering differing amounts of protection.

♦ **Cosmetic.** These sunglasses are lightly tinted and should only be worn in indirect sunlight. The lenses typically block only 70 percent of the sun's damaging rays, inviting damage, as well as fatigue and headaches.

♦ **General purpose.** Because they block 95 percent of UV light, these glasses are suitable for most outdoor activities. But if your eyes are sun-sensitive, you may need the maximum protection provided by special purpose sunglasses.

♦ **Special purpose.** These glasses offer maximum protection, blocking 99 percent of UV light. They are recommended for very bright environments, such as tropical beaches. Many eye specialist consider them the only smart option.

In addition, there are a number of lens types. There are quite a few "looks" to choose from.

♦ **Colored.** Note than color typically has little bearing on the ability of the lens to block harmful UV light.

♦ **Polarized.** These sunglasses are designed to protect your eyes from excessive brightness and surface glare, by filtering out light reflected off water, sand and snow.

♦ **Mirrored.** While these lenses reflect both light and heat, most offer little or no protection against UV light.

♦ **Photochromatic.** These sunglasses are light-sensitive, so they automatically adjust to the amount of light you are in. They typically require five or six exposures to different intensities of light before they will work properly.

Are you sun-sensitive?

You may be if you are taking one or more of the following "photo-sensitive" medications. These drugs can increase your skin's sensitivity to the sun—making you more likely to burn after a shorter period of exposure.

Acne medicine
tretinoin (Retin-A)

Diuretics
acetazolamine (Diamox)
amiloride (Midamor)
chlorothiazide (Diuril)
furosemide (Lasix)
hydrochlorothiazide (HydroDiuril)
methyclothiazide (Enduron)
metolazone (Zaroxolyn)
thiazides (Maxide, Dyazide)

Anti-cancer drugs
dacarbazine (DTIC-Dome)
fluorouracil (Flouroplex)
methotrexate (Mexate)
procarbazine (Matulane)
vinblastine (Velban)

Antidepressants
amitriptyline (Elavil)
amoxapine (Asendin)
desipramine (Norpramin)
doxepin (Adapin, Sinequan)
imipramine (Tofranil)
maprotiline (Ludiomil)
nortriptyline (Aventyl, Pamelor)

protriptyline (Vivactil)
trimipramine (Surmontil)

Diabetic drugs
acetohexamide (Dymelor)
chlorpropamide (Diabinese)
glipizide (Glucotrol)
glyburide (DiaBeta, Micronase)
tolazamide (Tolinase)
tolbutamide (Orinase)

Pain and inflammation
indomethicin (Indocin)
ketoprofen (Orudis)
meclofenamate (Meclomen)
naproxen (Naprosyn, Anaprox)
piroxicam (Feldene)
sulindac (Clinoril)

Antihistamines
astemizole (Hismanal)
chlorpheniramine (Chlor-Trimeton)
cyproheptadine (Periactin)
diphenhydramine (Benadryl)

Antibiotics
ciprofloxacin (Cipro)
doxycycline (Vibramycin)
griseofulvin (Fulvicin)
minocycline (Minocin)
nalidixic acid (NegGram)
sulfadoxine-pyrimethamine (Fansidar)
sulfamethoxazole (Gantanol)
sulfamethoxazole-trimethoprim (Bactrim, Septra)
sulfasalazine (Azulfidine)
tetracycline (Sumycin, Achromycin)

Antipsychotic drugs
chlorpromazine (Thorazine)
fluphenazine (Prolixin)

haloperidol (Haldol)
perphenazine (Trilafon)
prochlorperazine (Compazine)
promethazine (Phenergan)
thioridazine (Mellaril)
thiothixene (Navane)
trifluoperazine (Stelazine)
triflupromazine (Vesprin)
trimeprazine (Temaril)

Other drugs/chemicals
amiodarone (Cordarone)
bergamot oil, citron oil,
   lavender, lime, cedar,
   (in perfumes/cosmetics)
captopril (Capoten)
carbamazepine (Tegretol)
disopyramide (Norpace)
hexaclorophene (Phisohex)
isotretinon (Accutane)
6-methylcoumarin (in perfumes,
   shaving lotions)
musk ambrette (perfumes)
quinidine
coal tar solutions

How to treat a sunburn

The more anxious you are to enjoy your first day at the beach, the more likely you are to overdo it in the sun. So what do you do when you detect that rosy glow beginning to bloom on your back?

In the two to six hours after overexposure to the sun, you'll begin to know the full extent of the damage. Severe burns may be accompanied by itching, nausea, fever and chills. If a burn is severe or covers more than 25 percent of your body, consult a doctor. The good news is the burn peaks 11 to 24 hours later.

Here are some tips for preventing further damage and making yourself as comfortable as possible while you wait it out.

Cold compresses. A cold (but not ice cold) compress may prevent skin damage within the first four hours after overexposure to the sun. Cold water also relieves the heat and sting of a burn.

Local anesthetics. Americaine, Dermoplast, Foille and Solarcaine are effective in reducing sunburn pain for about 30 to 45 minutes. They should be used no more than four times a day. Americaine and Dermoplast are the strongest local anesthetics on the market. Foille and Solarcaine also contain antimicrobials to help prevent infection.

Moisturizers. Cocoa butter, will add moisture to sunburned skin to reduce dryness and possibly prevent significant peeling. Never apply butter or greasy ointments to sunburned skin. This will only further irritate the burn.

Anti-itch medications. Hydrocortisone Cream 1% or Benadryl Cream are effective when used as directed. They can be used along with local anesthetics.

Aspirin/analgesics. Some experts recommend taking 600mg to 650mg of aspirin as soon as possible after sun exposure to prevent the delayed phase of a sunburn. Repeat this dosage every two hours for up to six doses. If you are sensitive or allergic to aspirin, or take prescription drugs such as probenecid, methotrexate, coumadin, or other aspirin compounds, take Tylenol or another nonaspirin analgesic as directed to control sunburn pain.

Oatmeal. Sprinkle a cup of instant oatmeal into a cool bath and soak. Your skin will feel cooler and less irritated.

Home remedies. Many Florida residents claim a cool sponge bath made from tea brewed from tea bags will relieve sunburn pain.

Fluids. Drink plenty of fluids to avoid dehydration.

If you do go back out into the sun with sunburned skin, always use a sunscreen with an SPF of 30 or higher and reapply it frequently to prevent further damage to your skin by the sun.

The myth of the artificial tan

There are several different kinds of products that promise to give you a "quick" tan—or the illusion of a deeper, darker tan.

Tanning accelerators. These cosmetic products claim to stimulate a deeper, darker tan using tyrosine, an amino acid necessary for production of melanin. Current studies suggest that the effectiveness of these products is questionable at best.

Quick-tan products. Some of these products are taken orally. Others are applied directly to your skin. The FDA has not yet approved oral tanning products, so their safety is questionable. Topical products are nothing more than chemical dyes that stain the fat cells of your skin. Be careful applying them. Patches of dry skin tend to absorb more of the product so your "tan" may appear uneven at best, blotchy at worst. Most importantly, these products won't protect you from damaging rays when you do go out in the sun.

Are tanning beds and booths safer than the sun?

When used properly, tanning beds and booths should emit only UV-A rays. The goal is to tan without the risk of sunburn caused by UV-B rays. For this reason, manufacturers and tanning salon proprietors claim that indoor tanning is safer than sunlight. But no long-term studies have yet proven them right.

In fact, some tanning beds have been found to produce more than five times as much UV light as sunlight. And salon operators are not required to have any sort of special training.

Why risk premature aging or cancer? It's best to take the advice of many medical authorities and leave them alone.

Now that you're comfortable—and safe—in the sun, it's time to take a dip. Turn the page to learn what you need to know to stay in the swim.

IN SUMMARY....

☑ Excessive exposure to the sun's ultraviolet (UV) rays can cause permanent damage to your skin as well as the retina or cornea of your eyes. A sunscreen and good pair of sunglasses are essential equipment whenever you plan to spend time in the sun.

☑ Skin Protection Factor or SPF multiplies your skin's natural protection.

☑ Most people don't apply enough sunscreen. About one ounce is necessary to protect your entire body.

☑ Apply sunscreen even if the sky is overcast or you are sitting in the shade.

☑ A number of prescription drugs can make your skin more sensitive to the sun, increasing your chances of getting a sunburn. Check the list in this chapter and enlist your doctor or pharmacist in purchasing the right level of SPF protection.

☑ Waterproof sunscreen will stay on your skin twice as long as regular sunscreen and longer than water-resistant products. Sweat-resistant sunscreens will stay on for up to 30 minutes even if you are perspiring heavily.

☑ There are number of remedies for the heat and pain of a sunburn, including cold compresses, local anesthetics, anti-itch medications, aspirin or analgesics and oatmeal baths.

☑ Tanning acclerators, quick-tan products or tanning beds or booths make a variety of unverified claims. It is best to stay away from them.

Chapter 7

Safety in the swim

Headed for the beach? Whether you plan to practice your breaststroke or just cool off from that torrid bestseller, you should be watching for a few things other than a fin. Dangerous rip currents, the sting of a jellyfish, even a case of swimmer's ear can ruin an otherwise delightful afternoon. Here's how to keep them at bay.

Swimming in the ocean

Before you dip a toe in the water on any beach, find out whether the area is shark-infested, polluted or prone to rip currents.

Rip currents. According to the U.S. Lifesaving Association, underwater rip currents (bands of water that move seaward quickly) are especially hazardous because you can't see them. They can even occur in calm waters. If you get caught in one, don't struggle. Swim with it and try to angle into calm water as you signal for help.

Jellyfish and man-of-war stings. Even if you plan to just stroll along the beach—steer clear of that clear or beige-white umbrella-like "glob" of jelly, or you may be in for a painful sting. The potent poison in the long tentacles of a jellyfish can strike even after the creature has washed up on shore.

If you venture into deeper water, watch for the bright-blue, balloon-like man-of-war—although strong currents and storms sometimes ferry them into shallow water or even ashore.

If you are stung, the pain you feel may be faint or severe. Often, it is accompanied by a raised, itchy, red rash. Severe stings can cause headaches, muscle cramps, shortness of breath, nausea, coughing and even vomiting. If these symptoms persist or worsen, contact a doctor. In order to relieve the sting, take the following steps:

1. **Rinse the wound immediately**. Use sea water, never fresh water. It will activate the stinging cells! And never rub the wound.

2. **Apply rubbing alcohol** to neutralize the stinging cells in the wound. If rubbing alcohol isn't available, any alcohol will do, including wine and liquor.

3. **Remove jellyfish tentacles from your skin.** If jellyfish tentacles become stuck in your skin, follow the first two steps. Then, use gloves or a towel to apply a paste of sea water and baking soda to the wound. After five minutes, you can try to gently scrape the tentacles off with a knife or other sharp instrument. If you have access to a razor, you can coat the tentacles with shaving cream and gently shave them off.

4. **Apply meat tenderizer**. Meat tenderizer contains an enzyme that renders the poison inactive and prevents the stinging cells from rupturing on your skin. Household vinegar may also be effective when applied to man-of-war stings.

5. **Apply a topical analgesic spray.** If the pain persists, Dermoplast, Solarcaine or Americaine offer relief. Also take Tylenol as directed.

6. **Use an antihistamine.** Benadryl is a good choice to relieve itching.

Freshwater foes

If you're traveling to Africa, the Middle East, Asia, South America or the Caribbean, think twice before plunging into that clear-blue, freshwater lake. It may be infested with a parasite that causes Schistosomiasis, commonly known as "swimmer's itch."

Swimmer's itch is so common that the World Health Organization ranks it as one of the most prevalent diseases in the world. If you share the water with this minute creature, it will bore into your skin, causing intense itching that can last for several hours. Here's how to avoid it:

♦ **Don't rely on the word of locals.** They may insist the water is uncontaminated.

♦ **Sit on a beach towel or mat.** Even the sand beaches of developing countries may contain parasites that can penetrate your skin.

♦ **Swim in the ocean or hotel pool.** As a rule of thumb, if you can smell chlorine on your skin, the water is safe for swimming. Make sure ocean water is not polluted.

♦ **How to treat it.** If you think you've been swimming in contaminated waters, dry your skin by rubbing it vigorously with a towel and wash with rubbing alcohol.

What is "swimmer's ear"?

No matter where you swim—even if you shower every day or wash your hair over a sink—you can unknowingly trap water in your ears. This often leads to a common infection known as "swimmer's ear."

If one or both ears begin to itch; the ear canal becomes swollen and painful; you notice drainage from one or both ears, or the gland in your neck becomes swollen and painful, see a doctor.

If you have excessively dry and scaly ears, place a few drops of mineral oil or baby oil into each ear before swimming to prevent bacteria from taking hold and growing. Use Star Otic and Swim-Ear, both sold over the counter, after swimming to clear any trapped water. To remove trapped water follow these recommendations of the American Academy of Otolaryngology-Head and Neck Surgery:

1. Tilt your head so the affected ear is facing upward.

2. Pull gently on the lobe of your ear to clear any excess moisture.

3. Place a few drops of rubbing alcohol into the ear canal, using an eye dropper.

4. Wiggle your ear to make the alcohol goes all the way in.

5. Tilt your the head downward after a few seconds, to let the excess rubbing alcohol drain out.

6. Tap your head gently to make sure all of the alcohol drains out.

7. Never use sweet oil or olive oil to remove water from the ear.

8. Don't remove ear wax. It contains friendly bacteria and acts as a natural barrier to other bacteria.

9. Don't clear your ear canal with a hair pin or any other object. You could scratch or cut the delicate skin inside the ear canal, providing a place for bacteria to grow.

On those days when you're not in the water, you'll still want to keep cool, especially if you're visiting a hot, humid climate. Turn to the next chapter for help on living with the heat.

IN SUMMARY...

☑ Before you swim at any beach, find out whether the area is shark-infested, polluted or prone to rip currents.

☑ If you are stung by a jelly-fish or man-of-war, rinse the wound with sea water, never fresh water. Then apply rubbing alcohol or even liquor.

☑ Schistosomiasis, commonly known as "swimmer's itch" is caused by parasites found in freshwater lakes and streams as well as on sandy beaches in many developing countries.

☑ Meat tenderizer contains an enzyme that deactivates the poison of a sting and prevents the stinging cells from rupturing on your skin.

☑ If the pain persists, apply a topical analgesic spray, such as Dermoplast, Solarcaine or Americaine and take Tylenol as directed. An antihistamine, such as Benadryl, can also relieve the itching.

☑ If jellyfish tentacles become stuck to your skin, apply a paste of sea water and baking soda to the wound and gently scrape the tentacles off with a knife or other sharp instrument. You can also coat them with shaving cream and gently shave them off.

☑ If you get caught in a rip current, do not struggle. Swim with it and signal for help as you try to angle into calm water.

☑ Most hotel pools are safe for swimming as long as they are properly chlorinated and well maintained. As a rule of thumb, if you can smell chlorine on your skin, the water is safe for swimming.

☑ Swimmer's ear is a bacterial infection caused after water becomes trapped in your ear canal. Use Star Otic and Swim-Ear, sold over the counter, afterward to remove trapped water.

Chapter 8

Keeping your cool

Whether you're spending December in Australia or July in Florida, you're likely to find yourself braving a few warm, sticky afternoons. If you try to do too much sightseeing or get caught up in the friendly competition of a tennis match, you may not realize how much stress you're putting on your system.

Even if you're in great shape, overdoing it in hot, humid climates can lead to the discomfort of heat rash or to life-threatening heat stroke. Here are some tips for keeping your cool for an enjoyable and healthy trip. You won't feel the heat as much—or miss out on any activities—if you follow these guidelines.

- ♦ **Plan activities for morning and evening.** Begin the day with a sightseeing excursion, then head for the pool or an air-conditioned mall from 11 a.m. to 3 p.m.—the hottest part of the day.

- ♦ **Wear light-colored, loose-fitting clothing.**

- ♦ **Drink plenty of liquids.** Especially if you're exercising (that includes sightseeing). One hour before exercising, drink 8 to 16 ounces of water. Continue to drink 8 ounces of water at least every half-hour while you're exercising. If you're sightseeing or at the beach, take along a refillable plastic water bottle.

- ♦ **Replace electrolytes.** Drink Gatorade or eat potassium-rich tomatoes, bananas and oranges to replace electrolytes lost through perspiration.

- ♦ **Don't drink alcohol.** It may be tempting to have a cold beer after a game of tennis or midway through a game of golf, but it will only dehydrate you more.

How humidity turns it up

High temperatures that combine with high humidity can pack a wallop. The Heat Index on the next page will give you an idea of what the temperature outside really feels like when the humidity goes up.

	Heat Index Percent Humidity				
	50%	60%	70%	80%	90%
T 100°	120°	132°	144°		
E 95°	107°	114°	124°	136°	
M 90°	96°	100°	106°	113°	122°
P 85°	88°	90°	93°	97°	102°
80°	81°	82°	85°	86°	88°
75°	75°	76°	77°	78°	79°

How to treat heat rash and prickly heat

Heat rash appears in areas of your body that are prone to sweating and chafing, such as your underarms, neck, behind your knees or on your inner thighs. If the rash becomes inflamed, causing itching and stinging, it is called "prickly heat." Here's how to ease the discomfort.

♦ **Retire to a cool, dry place.** Air-conditioning helps lower the humidity as well as the temperature, so you'll stop perspiring.

♦ **Don't cover the rash.** Let the open air heal it. If you must cover the area, choose loose-fitting, lightweight, well-ventilated clothing that won't rub against the skin.

♦ **Bathe often.** Or take sponge baths at least twice a day. Aveeno Oatmeal Bath dissolved in a tub of warm water may help soothe the discomfort.

♦ **Use talcum powder.** It will keep the rash dry and reduce uncomfortable chafing, especially in places where your skin rubs together, such as your inner thighs.

♦ **Don't use chemicals.** Perfume, after-shave, cologne and makeup may irritate the area more.

If you get dehydrated

If you become dehydrated, try the following fluid duo:

1. In one glass, mix orange, apple or grapefruit juice with a half-teaspoon of honey and a pinch of salt.

2. In the other, mix water or a soft drink with one-fourth teaspoon of baking soda.

3. Alternate drinking from each glass until your thirst is quenched.

How to spot and treat heat illness

There are three basic types of heat illness that can literally stop you in your tracks while traveling.

Heat cramps. If you become aware of sudden sharp pains in your legs, arms or stomach accompanied by excessive sweating, take a break immediately. These "heat cramps" signal a lack of electrolytes or salt. Even if you've been drinking enough water, you've been losing salt through perspiration.

Relax in a cool place. Massage your cramped muscles. Drink fruit juice (orange, apple or grapefruit) mixed with a half-teaspoon of honey and a pinch of table salt to replace lost electrolytes.

Heat exhaustion. This more serious form of heat illness usually affects middle-aged people who over-exert themselves. When salt and water are lost through perspiration, your body temperature can rise. Your skin may become pale and feel clammy. Other symptoms include excessive perspiring, headache, weakness and dizziness.

Use the same treatment prescribed for heat cramps. You may also apply a cold, moist towel to your forehead. Return to normal activity gradually. In serious cases, you may have to visit an emergency room.

Heat stroke. If your body temperature reaches 104 degrees or higher, your life is in danger. The symptoms of heat stroke are similar to the symptoms of heat exhaustion, except that your heart may also be racing and instead of perspiring, your skin will usually be dry to the touch. Seek prompt medical attention.

Ready for a cool breeze? In the next chapter, we'll head for some high-altitude destinations.

IN SUMMARY...

☑ Plan sightseeing excursions for the cooler parts of the day, before 11 a.m. and after 3 p.m.

☑ Drink liquids before, during and after exercising in hot, humid weather to replace water and electrolytes you'll lose through perspiration. If you're sightseeing or at the beach, take along a refillable plastic water bottle.

☑ Wear light-colored, loose-fitting clothing.

☑ Keep areas affected by heat rash or inflamed "prickly heat" clean, dry and uncovered, if possible.

☑ Perfume, makeup, cologne, or after-shave will irritate the area more.

☑ If you notice sudden sharp pains in your legs, arms or stomach accompanied by excessive sweating, you may have heat cramps. Relax in a cool place. Massage your cramped muscles and replace lost electrolytes by drinking fruit juice mixed with a pinch of salt.

☑ If your temperature rises, your skin becomes pale and feels clammy and you are perspiring heavily, you may be suffering from heat exhaustion. Rest, drink fluids and apply a cold, damp towel to your forehead.

☑ If you must cover the area, choose only loose-fitting, lightweight, and well-ventilated clothing that won't rub against the skin.

☑ If your body temperature reaches 104 degrees or more, your heart is racing and your skin is dry to the touch, seek prompt medical attention for heat stroke.

Chapter 9

The lowdown on high-altitude travel

Whether you are scaling the ruins near Mexico City or skiing the slopes at Aspen, you're likely to encounter another common traveler's malady called altitude sickness.

Also known as mountain sickness, altitude sickness affects about one in four travelers to destinations 5,000 feet or more above sea level. In these lofty spots, the air that often seems to be so much clearer and cleaner than the air you left behind is also quite a bit "thinner"—meaning there is less oxygen to breathe.

You're likely to feel symptoms similar to the symptoms of jet lag—fatigue, headaches, nausea and difficulty sleeping the first few days.

The high spots. If you're a skier or hiker, you'll recognize many of the following destinations (listings include altitude in feet).

The United States

Aspen, Colorado	7,773
Butte, Montana	6,765
Cheyenne, Wyoming	6,101
Colorado Springs, Colorado	6,980
Flagstaff, Arizona	6,900
Laramie, Wyoming	7,272
Santa Fe, New Mexico	6,950
West Yellowstone, Montana	6,645

Central and South America

Bogota, Colombia	8,878
Guanajuata, Mexico	8,202
Mexico City, Mexico	7,347
Pachuca, Mexico	7,859
Puebla, Mexico	7,094
Toluca, Mexico	8,793
Zacatecas, Mexico	8,025

Europe

Chamonix, France	12,486
Zermatt, Switzerland	5,314

Asia

Darjeeling, India	7,431

Africa

Nairobi, Kenya	5,450

How to avoid altitude sickness

The only way to get immediate relief is to descend to a lower altitude. Here are some tips on minimizing the symptoms of altitude sickness until your body has time to get acclimated to your new conditions.

- **Take the scenic route.** That's another way of saying ascend slowly. If possible, travel no more than 2,000 feet a day at elevations of 5,000 to 10,000 feet, and 1,000 feet a day between 10,000 to 15,000 feet. Your body will gradually grow accustomed to changes in the atmosphere.

- **Slow down.** Avoid vigorous sightseeing or strenuous exercise for the first few days after you arrive.

- **Consult a doctor.** If you suffer from a heart condition, circulatory or respiratory disease, get your doctor's okay to visit any destination above 5,000 feet.

The ski report

If you're a skier or winter sports enthusiast, you may face a few other challenges once you hit the slopes.

Frostbite. When you're out all afternoon in high winds and low temperatures, you may not realize that the exposed skin tissue on the surface of your cheeks, nose and ears is beginning to freeze. The longer you brave frigid temperatures, the more blood your body diverts away from the surface of your skin and your extremities, such as fingers and toes, to maintain the constant temperature necessary for the function of your vital organs.

In effect, your body may choose to sacrifice some body parts to frostbite to keep you from freezing to death. Here's how to keep things from going that far.

Several factors can predispose you to frostbite. If you're going to be out in the cold for long, take these precautions:

- **Dress in layered clothing.** This allows ventilation and reduces perspiration.

- **Stay dry.** Perspiration or moisture from falling snow can bind the cold to your skin. If you feel your fingers or ears freezing, never rub them with snow. This will not increase blood flow to the area. It will only cause more freezing.

- **Stay active.** This will keep as much blood as possible flowing to every part of your body. If your feet do become frostbitten, however, don't try to walk on them.

- **Take frequent breaks**. Be sure to come inside to warm up every hour or so, especially when it's windy or extremely cold.

♦ **Drink plenty of liquids.** Dehydration can make you more prone to frostbite. But don't drink alcohol until you're ready to call it a day. Alcohol will cause your body to lose heat and may impair your judgment about the condition of your body.

♦ **Avoid smoking.** The nicotine in cigarettes causes blood vessels to constrict, decreasing blood flow.

To treat frostbite, warm the frostbitten part promptly. Use lukewarm, not hot, water in a container that is large enough to allow free movement. A pink flush should return to the extreme tip of the affected part in about 30 minutes.

Soak the injured part daily. Use a whirlpool bath to soak the frostbitten part at least twice a day until healing is complete.

Don't thaw a frostbitten part if there is a chance it might re-freeze. A second freeze will increase the injury significantly. As always, seek medical attention immediately if complications arise.

Other high-altitude concerns

Sunburn. The closer you are to the sun, the more intense its burning rays. Add glare, caused by reflection off the snow and you have a prescription for sunburn. For a complete guide to preventing and treating sunburn, review Chapter 6.

Chapped lips. Low humidity combined with cold, whipping winds can give you painfully dry, chapped lips. Use a lip balm. Chapstick is probably the most familiar of these products, formulated to be thick and waxy to prevent you from licking it off. Be sure that any product you try has a sunscreen with an SPF of 15.

Products like Blistex help kill pain while protecting chapped lips from further damage. Carmex, contains a moisturizer to soothe and protect damaged lips.

Tips for hikers and sightseers

Whatever the altitude, if you spend a lot of time seeing the sights or tackling challenging trails, you don't want any of the following minor annoyances to slow you down.

Blisters. New shoes can rub and press on the heels or balls of your feet or your toes, causing a fluid-filled blister.

To avoid blisters, invest in a good pair of walking shoes. Properly fitting shoes or hiking boots are a must for any traveler. But don't wait to break them in on the first day of your trip. Begin wearing new shoes or boots for an hour a day, gradually adding time until they feel comfortable.

Wear socks. Cotton or woolen socks are best. If you plan to do a lot of walking invest in padded runner's socks or wear two pairs of socks, with a dusting of talcum powder between.

If you do end up with a blister, cushion it with a moleskin cloth. Place a moleskin (available in the foot care section of your pharmacy) around the blister to ease the pain and protect it from further friction while walking. If moleskin isn't available, place a couple of band-aids over the blister until it heals.

Resist the urge to burst it. The fragile "bubble" covering a blister provides a natural barrier against infection. If you burst it, you may get more trouble than you bargained for. However, if you are intent on this course of action, carefully follow this step-by-step procedure:

1. **Cleanse** the blister with 70% isopropyl alcohol.

2. **Puncture** the blister with a sterilized needle or pin at three or four distinct sites.

3. **Drain** all of the accumulated fluid by pressing on the blister gently with a sanitary cloth.

4. **Apply** a triple antibiotic ointment to the blister.

5. **Cover** the area with a sterile bandage.

6. **Clean** the area as often as possible until the skin has healed.

Sore muscles. Whatever the activity, if you overdo, your body will tell you so in no uncertain terms. Sore muscles can be a nuisance while traveling. Here's how to make sure they don't bother you.

Start an exercise program. One or two months before your trip, begin to exercise those muscles you expect to use while you're traveling. That may mean walking or stair-climbing. If you plan to carry a backpack or an extensive array of camera equipment, be to sure exercise your arms, back and stomach using free weights or calisthenics.

Before you start out each day, take a few moments to limber up. If you'll be doing a lot of walking, try these four stretching exercises. Hold each stretch for a minimum of 15 seconds for each leg.

1. **The runner's stretch.** Lean into a wall or place your hands on a stable surface, such as a table or chair. Extend the heel of one foot and bend the knee of the front leg.

2. **Achilles stretch.** Then, bend the knee of the extended leg to stretch the Achilles tendon.

3. **Quadricep stretch.** Balancing yourself against a wall or chair, if necessary, lift the heel of one foot as far behind you as you can, keeping it close to your body.

4. **Ankle stretch.** Rotate each ankle clockwise for 10 counts, then counter-clockwise for another 10.

Whenever you feel tired or sore, look for a place to rest. When you're ready to get started again, repeat your stretching exercises.

If you do end up over-exerting yourself and find yourself sore the next day, here are a few suggestions for treating those aching muscles:

1. **Take a warm bath.** Even if you feel too tired when you return to your room, soak in a warm bath. Continue to massage and stretch your aching muscles.

2. **Rub an ointment,** such as Myoflex, into sore muscles.

3. **Indulge in a massage.** If you are on a cruise ship or visiting a resort, schedule this as a treat. Or persuade your husband or wife to massage your tired muscles.

4. **Keep going.** Unless you become completely immobilized, push onward—at a slower pace. Much of the stiffness and soreness you feel when you wake up in the morning will go away as the blood begins to flow in your legs.

You may not be able to move fast enough to escape the bugs, however. In the next chapter, we'll talk about how to enjoy a trip free of stings, bites and more serious diseases.

IN SUMMARY...

☑ Altitude sickness, often mistaken for jet lag or general traveler's fatigue, affects one in four travelers to destinations 5,000 feet or more above sea level. Among its symptoms are fatigue, headaches, nausea and difficulty in sleeping.

☑ You can "cure" altitude sickness by descending immediately to a lower altitude. Prevent it by ascending slowly—2,000 feet a day at elevations of 5,000 to 10,000 feet, and 1,000 feet a day when you reach elevations of 10,000 to 15,000 feet.

☑ Avoid vigorous sightseeing or strenuous exercise for the first few days after you arrive.

☑ If you suffer from a heart condition, circulatory or respiratory disease, consult your doctor before visiting any destination higher than 5,000 feet.

☑ Frostbite is frozen skin tissue, usually found on the surface of the skin or extremities, where blood flow can be reduced over long periods of exposure to cold temperatures.

☑ Wet clothing, exposed body parts, dehydration and exhaustion are invitations to frostbite. If the weather is cold, remain active and wear many layers of clothing to prevent perspiration buildup.

☑ If you get frostbite, warm the part promptly in lukewarm—not hot—water until a pink flush returns. Then soak the injured part for 20 minutes twice a day in a whirlpool bath until healing is complete.

☑ Alcohol causes your body to lose heat. Nicotine constricts the blood vessels, decreasing blood flow to extremities.

☑ Don't attempt to thaw a frostbitten part if there is a chance it might re-freeze. A second freeze greatly increases the injury.

☑ Protect your lips from chapping with a balm or chapstick with an SPF of 15. Blistex, contains a local anesthetic and Carmex contains a moisturizer to sooth and protect damaged lips.

☑ If you plan to do a lot of walking or hiking, invest in a pair of properly fitting shoes or hiking boots. Don't wait to break in a new pair of shoes on your trip.

☑ Wear cotton or wool socks. If you'll be doing a lot of walking, invest in padded socks or wear two pairs, with a dusting of talcum powder between.

☑ Cover a blister with a mole-skin cloth or a couple of band-aids to ease pain and protect it from further friction.

☑ Regularly exercise the muscles you expect to use while you're traveling a month or so before you depart.

☑ Stretch before you start out each day, when you rest and before turning in for the day.

☑ Take a warm bath, apply ointment or schedule a professional massage to ease the pain of aching muscles.

Chapter 10

How to keep the bugs from bugging you

Whether you're strolling along a deserted beach on an exotic island, seeing the sights in a world-class city or camping in the wilds...you can expect company. The cloud of ravenous mosquitos that descends at dusk, the insistent bee trying to light on top of your cola can, the tiny tick clinging to your ankle after an innocent hike in the woods.

Most of the time, a good repellent is all you need to keep bugs from bugging you. To make sure you're not bothered by bites and stings, or at risk for more dangerous diseases, such as malaria or Lyme disease, read on for what you'll need to know to deal with every contingency.

Choosing—and using— insect repellent

Here are some tips on how to select and use an insect repellent that will deter most pests.

◆ **Choose a product containing 30-percent DEET.** Short for N, N-diethyltoluamide, this is the repellent of choice among most experts. According to Richard Pollack, of the Harvard School of Public Health, products with more than 30-percent DEET are *less* rather than more effective.

◆ **Cover, but don't saturate, your skin and clothes.** Holding a spray container upright, six to eight inches from your skin, spray with a slow, sweeping motion.

◆ **Apply repellent to your face with your hands.** Then spray some repellent into your hand and spread it on your face or neck, carefully avoiding your eyes, mouth and nostrils.

◆ **For maximum protection, spread the repellent on exposed skin by hand.** As an alternative, Skin-So-Soft by Avon repels most insects, including deer ticks—while it gives you silky, smooth skin.

♦ **Spray the cuffs and socks.** Especially if you plan to hike off a trail, spray all openings in your clothing to protect areas from ticks and chiggers.

♦ **Keep insect repellent with you.** Reapply it as necessary, especially after sweating.

How to prevent bee stings

Bees and other stinging insects leave their "calling card" behind—painfully implanting a barbed stinger into your skin. The attached sack will continue to pump venom into the skin for up to three minutes more.

Be careful what you eat and drink. Stinging insects are attracted by the sweet smell and taste of many foods and beverages. Always look before you take a sip or a bite. If you see an insect buzzing around the top of an aluminum can, for example, pour the contents into a clear glass. More than a few people have accidentally swallowed insects—with fatal result.

In addition, don't wear scented products. This includes perfumes and most hair sprays and cosmetics. Wear light or subdued colors. Black or red clothing attracts stinging insects.

If you are stung...

♦ **Stay calm.** Slowly move away from the area. Running or rapid movement may precipitate further attacks from more insects.

♦ **Immediately remove the stinger.** But take care not to squeeze the attached venom sac in your haste! This will only force more venom into your skin. The best method is to use an object with a flat edge, such as your fingernail or a credit card, to push the sac up from underneath. Almost immediately, the area will become red and swollen. It may also itch. You may also experience nausea, vomiting and diarrhea.

♦ **Wash** the area with warm, soapy water.

♦ **Apply** ice to relieve pain and swelling and prevent the further spread of the venom. Applying aspirin tablets directly to the sting may also help to relieve the pain and swelling.

♦ **Use** unseasoned meat tenderizer, if available, to deactivate the venom.

♦ **Reduce** the swelling and itching with an over-the-counter product, such as Benadryl cream and Hydro-cortisone cream 1%. Resist scratching since it can cause infection.

♦ **Relieve** pain by taking Tylenol as directed and using topical anesthetic, such as Solarcaine, Foille Spray, Dermoplast or Americaine. If your throat swells, you have difficulty breathing, a tight feeling in the chest and your blood pressure drops dramatically, you are having an allergic reaction to the sting. Death from a bee sting can occur in as little as five minutes. If you know you're allergic to bee stings, wear a medical ID bracelet or necklace. Carry a bee sting emergency kit and know how to use it. (Check the solution in your kit frequently. If it turns pinkish-brown, replace it.) Seek emergency medical treatment.

Chiggers

Most prevalent during the spring and summer, these tiny red bugs attach microscopic larva to your skin. The larva surrounds itself with a cover-like "tube," in which it continues to live and feed. The result is a red welt, much larger than a mosquito bite

To treat a chigger bite, you must first kill the chigger larva living in its makeshift "tube." Here's how:

♦ **Wash** the area thoroughly.

♦ **Apply** a product, such as Chiggerex, Chiggertox or Chigger-rid used as directed.

♦ **You may also paint** the tube with clear fingernail polish. This will suffocate the larva.

Mosquitoes

The exposed parts of the body (typically your face, neck, legs, arms) are fair game for mosquitoes. But these persistent pests can also bite through thin clothing. When they do, they release a salivary secretion that results in a small, red welt that itches. Take these steps to relieve itching:

♦ **Wash** the area with warm, soapy water daily.

♦ **Apply** Benadryl or Hydrocortisone 1% cream to relieve the itching.

♦ **Avoid** scratching mosquito bites. This can lead to an infection.

What you need to know about malaria

If you're embarking on a safari adventure in Africa or an extensive tour of Asia, you should take every precaution against this devastating disease. It is transmitted by infected Anopheles mosquitoes that introduce parasites into your bloodstream.

Malaria causes a high fever, headache, chills and fatigue. Left untreated, it attacks red blood cells and, over time, can cause damage to your liver, and even death. If you receive treatment and recover, you may cope with lingering effects of the disease for the rest of your life.

Areas where malaria is a threat

Africa
Algeria [C]
Angola [R]
Benin [R]
Botswana
Burkina Faso [R]
Burundi [R]
Cameroon [R]
Central African Republic [R]
Chad
Comoros Saotome
Congo [R]
Djibouti
Egypt
Ethiopia [R]
Gabon [R]
Gambia [R]
Ghana [R]
Guinea [R]
Ivory Coast [R]
Kenya [R]
Liberia
Libya [C]
Madagascar
Mali
Malawi [R]
Mauritania
Mauritius
Morocco [C]
Mozambique
Namibia
Niger
Nigeria [R]
Rwanda [R]
Senegal [R]

Sierra Leone
Somalia [R]
South Africa
Sudan [R]
Swaziland
Togo [R]
Tanzania [R]
Uganda [R]
Zaire [R]
Zambia
Zimbabwe

The Caribbean
Dominican Republic
Haiti

Central America
Belize
Costa Rica
El Salvador
Guatemala
Honduras
Mexico [H]
Nicaragua
Panama

The Middle East
Afghanistan
Bangladesh
Bhutan
India
Iran
Iraq
Maldives
Nepal

Oman
Pakistan
Saudi Arabia
Syria
Turkey
United Arab Emirates
Yemen

Polynesia and The South Pacific
New Guinea [R]
Solomon Islands
Vanuatu

South America
Bolivia
Brazil [R]
Colombia [R]
Ecuador [R]
French Guiana [R]
Guyana
Paraguay
Peru
Surinam [R]

Southeast Asia
Burma [R]
China [T]
Hong Kong
Indonesia [R]
Kampuchea [R]
Laos [R]
Philippines [R]
Thailand [R]
Vietnam [R]

Key to symbols

[C]: These areas are generally thought to be safe, however the International Association of Medical Assistance to Travelers (IAMAT) recommends preventive therapy if you plan to travel to infested areas.

[H] : Malaria prevention medication is recommended for hikers and campers along the coastal regions of these areas and for travelers who stay overnight at certain archaeological sites. All travelers, even those staying at major resorts, should use mosquito repellent after dark.

[R]: Mosquitos in these areas have shown resistance to chloroquine, once the most popular prescription medication used to prevent malaria. Request mefloquine (Lariam) or another alternative therapy.

[T]: If you plan to fly into major cities in these areas and take only daytime trips to the countryside, you don't need medication to prevent malaria.

How to prevent malaria

Take a prescription medication that prevents malaria before you depart. Chloroquine has long been the most effective way to prevent malaria. Take one dose a week before you depart for a high-risk area. Continue to take the medication weekly while you travel and for six weeks after you return home.

Many strains of malaria have become resistant to chloroquine in recent years. The U.S. Centers for Disease Control recommends that travelers to areas where malaria is known to be resistant to chloroquine (see the areas marked with the symbol [R] on the table in this chapter) substitute a drug called mefloquine (Lariam). Take one dose a week before you depart and continue taking it every week until four weeks after your return home. Mefloquine should be taken with food or milk and at least eight ounces of water. It is not recommended for people suffering from epilepsy. If you have a mental disorder or heart disease, make your doctor aware of this before taking mefloquine.

Other tips to reduce your risk of malaria:

♦ **Use** mosquito repellent with DEET.

♦ **Wear** clothes made of tightly woven material that cover most of your body while traveling.

♦ **Remain** in well-screened areas or near the center of trails and roads.

♦ **Sleep** under mosquito netting at night.

Ticks

The deer tick carries Lyme disease and can be found in more than 30 states, although it is most prevalent in New England, New York, the northern part of the Midwest and the northwestern states.

Most people bitten by an infected tick do not get sick. But for those who do get the disease, it can be devastating.

Lyme disease is difficult to diagnose because it has many symptoms. The first sign is usually a bull's eye-shaped rash that appears a few days to a few weeks after you're bitten. The rash does not always occur, however.

The rash may be preceded by flu-like symptoms, such as a headache, fever, muscle aches and a general lack of energy. Many people also feel pain, especially in the knee joint.

Early detection and diagnosis is extremely important. The disease can be treated effectively with antibiotics. If you suspect you may have Lyme disease, contact your doctor immediately.

In order to prevent tick bites, follow this advice:

♦ **Use** an insect repellent containing DEET on your clothing, as well as directly on your skin.

- ◆ **Wear** light-colored, tightly woven clothing.

- ◆ **Tuck** your pant legs into socks or shoes and tuck your shirt into your pants.

- ◆ **Stay** near the center of trails and roads.

- ◆ **Check** yourself—and your pets—frequently for ticks.

- ◆ **Remove** ticks immediately, using the following procedure.

How to remove a tick:

- ◆ **Use tweezers.** Grab the head of the tick as close to the skin as possible.

- ◆ **Pull upward.** Slowly and steadily, pull upward so that the tick is forced to open its mouth. Don't jerk, crush or puncture the tick during removal. This may cause infected parts of the tick to enter your bloodstream.

- ◆ **Wash the site**. Use soap and apply an antiseptic or topical antibiotic, such as Neosporin, to the area.

- ◆ **Save the tick**. Place it in a sealed jar, labeled with the date the tick was found and part of the body it was removed from. Take it to your doctor if you suspect you have Lyme Disease.

- ◆ **Caution:** Never use fingernail polish, gasoline, matches, oils or vaseline. These agents may leave tick parts in the skin and increase the risk of Lyme disease.

While you're busy eluding all these flying and crawling insects, watch where you're walking. That patch of green you just walked through could poison your good time—if it's poison ivy, oak or sumac, that is. In the next chapter, we'll look at how to steer clear of all three.

IN SUMMARY...

☑ The best way to prevent a sting or bite from an insect is to apply repellent containing DEET.

☑ Stinging insects are attracted by sweet foods and beverages. If you're outdoors, never take a sip or a bite without looking. If possible, pour beverages in aluminum cans into clear containers.

☑ Don't wear scented perfumes, hair spray or cosmetics. Avoid wearing black or red clothing.

☑ Resist scratching a sting or bite. You could cause an infection.

☑ If you are stung by a bee, remove its stinger immediately by forcing it out of the skin from underneath with a fingernail or flat edge of a credit card. Take care not to squeeze or rupture the attached venom sac.

☑ Ice or aspirin tablets, applied directly to the skin, can bring relief from the pain and swelling of a bee sting.

☑ If you are allergic to bee stings, wear a medical ID bracelet or necklace and always carry your emergency bee sting kit.

☑ Products such as Chiggerex, Chiggertox, or Chigger-rid will kill chigger larva. You can also suffocate them by painting over the entire area with clear fingernail polish.

☑ If you're traveling to an area in which malaria is a risk, begin taking a prescription drug such as chloroquine, or mefloquine before you depart and continue until after you return.

☑ While you're traveling in these areas, wear clothes made of tightly woven material that covers most of your body. Remain in well-screened areas and near the center of trails and roads. If possible, sleep under mosquito netting.

☑ Ticks that carry Lyme disease are most prevalent in the New England states, New York, the northern part of the Midwest and the northwestern states.

☑ Check yourself—and your pets—frequently for ticks. If you find a tick, remove it immediately using the procedure above.

☑ Early detection and diagnosis of Lyme disease is extremely important. It can be treated with antibiotics.

Chapter 11

Knowing your poison (ivy, oak and sumac, that is)

It's a beautiful afternoon. As you stroll along, you spot the perfect panorama...just off the trail and through a little bit of underbrush. Just push aside this hanging vine...and...there!

Whether you realize that you've just trekked through a patch of poison oak and pushed aside a flaming strand of poison ivy right away...or a few days later when the itchy rash starts to erupt on your hands and ankles, it's too late to remember that prevention is the best treatment.

Now, let's turn back the reel and take a look at what to watch out for on the trail.

How to recognize the three "sinister sisters"

Poison ivy. Watch bushes or rope-like climbing vines similar to ivy houseplants. The leaves grow in clusters of three. The shiny leaves are green in the spring and summer (May through July) and bright red

in the fall. From late summer to late fall, you may see small, smooth, white berries. The small, yellow flowers are the only nonpoisonous part of the plant. Poison ivy is especially abundant in the eastern part of the U.S. and in southeast Canada.

Poison oak. Shaped like the leaves of an oak tree, poison oak leaves are hairy and grow in clusters of three on a bush. The berries and flowers are similar in appearance to those found on poison ivy and follow the same growth cycle. Western poison oak is found along the Pacific Coast from Mexico all the way up into Canada. Eastern poison oak is found in a triangular area, from Texas to New Jersey and down through Florida, where the sandy soil is more conducive to its growth.

Poison sumac. Growing as a woody shrub or tree with pointed leaves in clusters of 7 to 13 leaves per stalk, poison sumac has dark, smooth bark. Its flowers are visible from May through July. You'll find white berries from August through November. It is typically found in the swamps of the southern and eastern U.S.

Steer clear of contact

Don't pet your pet. If you suspect your dog or cat has been strolling through poison ivy, oak or sumac, put on long-sleeves and a pair of rubber gloves and give it a good bath first.

Wash your hands. The oil on poison ivy, oak and sumac contains a toxin that can be spread further through touch.

Even dead plants still contain the toxic oils. Wash the affected skin with soap—preferably yellow laundry soap—immediately. Washing with plain water can spread the rash.

Launder your clothing. Immediately wash any clothing that may have contacted these plants. That includes your caps, socks and sneakers.

Never burn any of these plants. The toxin can get into your lungs or blanket your entire body causing a severe allergic reaction.

How to treat poison ivy, oak and sumac rashes

If you're like 70 percent of the North American population, you're likely to notice a red rash erupting on your hands, face or anywhere you spread the toxin two or three days after contact. The rash is usually streaked and spotty. It can be raised and filled with fluid. It is almost always characterized by intense itching. Touching the liquid in the sores of the rash will not spread it further.

The affected area will eventually dry up and the rash will disappear on its own, usually in about two or three weeks. Until then:

- ♦ **Avoid** scratching the rash. It may cause infection. And never burst the sores; they are protecting the underlying skin layers.

- ♦ **Apply** over-the-counter creams or ointments, such as Hydrocortisone 1% cream, Cortaid, Cortisone 10, Rhuli Cream, Ivy Rid or Ivy Dry three to four times a day to reduce the redness, swelling and itch. Although many of us grew up believing Calamine lotion is the best choice, it is not as effective as these products.

- ♦ **Take** an antihistamine, such as Benadryl to help control itching.

- ♦ **Relieve** itching and mild burning temporarily by using topical anesthetic products, such as Americaine, Solarcaine and Dermoplast.

- ♦ **Soak** in very cold or moderately hot water. If the rash covers a large area of your body, add Domeboro or Aveeno

Oatmeal Bath to temporarily relieve pain and itching.

Caution: If the rash is around your eyes, doesn't respond to over-the-counter products or seems to be spreading rapidly, contact your doctor.

Now that we've covered all the minor maladies you're likely to encounter while traveling, you can expect to be one healthy traveler. But do you need to be healthy to travel? In the next chapter, we'll open up a world of travel to anyone suffering from chronic illnesses and medical conditions.

IN SUMMARY...

☑ Learn to recognize poison ivy, oak and sumac, so you can easily spot them when you're outside. Remember, even dead plants can still cause a rash.

☑ Take an antihistamine to help control itching. Temporarily relieve itch and mild burning by applying topical anesthetics, such as Americaine, Solarcaine and Dermoplast, and soak in very cold or moderately hot water.

☑ Avoid scratching the rash. This can promote infection. And never burst the sores. They are protecting the underlying layers of skin.

☑ If you're sure you've come in contact with plant toxins, wash the affected areas immediately with soap, preferably yellow laundry soap. Washing with plain water can spread the rash.

☑ If you have any reason to suspect that your pet has been rolling around in poison ivy, oak or sumac, do not touch it without gloves until you have given it a bath.

☑ Launder any clothing after it has touched or contacted these plants—including caps, socks and sneakers.

☑ Over-the-counter creams or ointments, such as Hydrocortisone 1% cream, Cortaid, Cortisone 10, Rhuli Cream, Ivy Rid or Ivy Dry should be applied three to four times a day to reduce the redness, swelling and itching.

☑ If the rash is around your eyes, does not respond to over-the-counter products or seems to be spreading rapidly, contact your doctor.

Chapter 12

Traveling with health problems

If you're undergoing treatment for cancer, have a chronic heart condition or are under a doctor's care for a range of other medical problems, you don't have to retire to the role of "armchair traveler."

In fact, it may be possible for you to schedule chemotherapy treatments close to your travel destination. Or enjoy the diversion of many different destinations—while you relax in the stress-free environment of a cruise ship. In other words, if your travel spirit is willing (and after all, isn't that why you picked up this book?), then you should be able. All it takes is the help of your doctor and a little planning.

General guidelines for healthy travel

Have your doctor evaluate your travel fitness. Before you plan your travel itinerary, have a frank talk with your doctor. Your functional ability and the severity of your condition may preclude you from traveling by air or visiting a high-altitude destination. Your doctor may offer alternatives or prescribe protective guidelines. Don't commit to a travel schedule until you have your doctor's blessing.

Have a plan for medication. If you are a diabetic or are taking medication to control pain, it is essential to have a plan for getting through customs, adjusting your dosing schedule to a new time zone and replacing your prescription drugs in case they are lost are stolen. It's all covered in-depth in Chapter 2.

Locate medical resources. Your doctor can help you schedule chemotherapy or dialysis treatments at another treatment center and suggest medical resources you can access in case of an emergency.

Check your insurance coverage. Make sure you'll be covered while traveling, especially if you plan to spend time outside the United States. You'll find a step-by-step plan for sorting it out in Chapter 1.

Be prepared for an emergency. Subscribe to Medic Alert and carry important medical information with you, so you'll be properly cared for if you are unconscious or can't speak for yourself. Chapter 1 will get you started compiling a Healthy Traveler's Kit for most any situation. Ask your doctor for additional suggestions. For example, it may be a good idea to carry a baseline EKG with you if you have a history of heart attacks.

Ask about immunizations. If you have a respiratory disease, you may need additional immunizations against pneumonia or influenza. The vaccines necessary to travel in some countries may affect the medication you're currently taking. Your dosage may need to be adjusted.

Request special meals. Try to stick to the diet you follow at home. Although there is typically an abundance of fruits and vegetables to choose from on cruise ship buffets, airline meals can be a cardiovascular nightmare—loaded with fat, salt and cholesterol.

When you book your flight, or at least 24 hours before you're scheduled to depart, order a low-salt, low-cholesterol meal or diabetic meal. If you're traveling abroad, ask about the calorie and sugar content of foods you're not familiar with if you have diabetes. If you suffer from kidney disease, arrange for meals low in sodium, protein and potassium.

Relax. When your health is fragile, it's more important than ever to know your own limits. Try not to get upset over delays or anxious about missing scheduled events. Stress and anxiety may trigger an unnecessary health crisis. At the first sign of fatigue or anxiety, slow down or lay down. Moderation is your passport to enjoying your travel experience.

Now, let's look at how to travel with a number of specific medical conditions.

Cancer

Schedule chemotherapy while you're traveling. If you're currently undergoing regular chemotherapy that would conflict with your scheduled trip, your doctor can help you make arrangements to receive treatment at a cancer center near your destination. Do this well in advance of your departure.

To get the ball rolling, request a list of cancer centers throughout the country from your local cancer hospital or the American Cancer Society.

Cardiovascular conditions

Here are some precautions for any traveler who is being treated for heart disease, coronary artery disease, hypertension, or who has a history of heart attacks or strokes.

Know what to do in the event of heart attack. Watch for these two unmistakable symptoms:

♦ Pain in the chest, upper abdomen, or down the left arm and shoulder

♦ Extreme shortness of breath

These symptoms can occur together, but usually one is stronger than the other. Other symptoms may include dizziness, sweating, indigestion, nausea and vomiting, pale skin and/or bluish colored lips, skin and fingernails.

At the first sign of these symptoms go directly to a hospital emergency room. The sooner you get medical aid, the better your chance of controlling damage to your heart.

Refresh your nitroglycerin tablets. If they are more than six months old, replace them with a fresh supply before you leave.

Stay away from high-altitude destinations. Less oxygen in the air means you'll have a tougher time breathing and you'll feel more fatigued.

Stay inside during midday. If you'll be traveling to a hot, humid climate, plan to take an air-conditioned siesta from 11 a.m. to 3 p.m. each day. Even the healthiest hearts can be stressed by too much activity during this time.

Don't fly without permission from your doctor. If you've had a stroke, you should wait at least two weeks before flying, according to the American Medical Association. If you've had a heart attack, wait four weeks before flying. If you have a pacemaker, you'll probably set off most airport metal detectors. It's a good idea to let the airport personnel know ahead of time and carry a letter from your doctor.

Diabetes

Carry more insulin than you'll need. It's a good idea to have at least twice as much as you expect to use with you during your trip—especially if you'll be traveling outside the United States. U-100 insulin is not available in every country and some of your insulin may become unusable while you're traveling.

Carry a typed prescription for your syringes. Some states and foreign countries only sell syringes by prescription. If you carry syringes with you (and you should), also carry a letter from your doctor to speed you through airport security and customs.

Never carry pre-filled syringes. Inject only half as much air into the vial of insulin when using a syringe in flight to compensate for the difference in air pressure.

Refrigerate unopened insulin, if possible. If not, keep it in a cool place, especially if you'll be visiting a warm tropical climate. Regular insulin is good for 18 months. Lente is good for 24 months, and NPH is good for up to 36 months, stored at normal room temperature. Never use insulin if clumps have formed in it or it is discolored.

Carry a sugar source. Glucose gels, tablets or another sugar source will rescue you in case of an insulin reaction.

Kidney disease

If you're traveling with a kidney disease, such as nephrotic syndrome or chronic renal failure; have had a kidney transplant; are on extensive drug therapy or renal dialysis, take the following precautions.

Don't travel far from a hospital with a hemodialysis unit. Most large "destination" cities have excellent dialysis centers. Some cruises are specifically designed and equipped for individuals with kidney disorders. A list of worldwide dialysis facilities is available from *Dialysis and Transplantation Magazine* (818-782-7328). Ask your doctor for a list of kidney specialists, in case of an emergency.

Schedule dialysis treatments. This should be done at least two to three months in advance of travel.

Respiratory diseases

Here are special precautions for travelers with emphysema, chronic bronchitis, asthma, cystic fibrosis or chronic obstructive pulmonary disease.

Plan for different climates. If you have emphysema, asthma or chronic bronchitis, cold air can precipitate bronchial spasms. Hot air, whether humid or dry, also can cause problems for people with emphysema or chronic bronchitis. Asthmatics should avoid known allergens, especially in tropical climates.

Carry more inhalers than you'll need. Asthmatics should be prepared with inhalers.

Test your inhaler to determine how full the canister is by placing it in water. If it sinks, it is full. The more it floats, the emptier it is.

Replace canisters that are nearly empty before leaving home.

Clean all inhalers and breathing equipment frequently, using warm soapy water. This is especially important in tropical climates. Make sure the tap water is safe or use purified or bottled water to clean your equipment. (See Chapter 5 for instructions on how to purify contaminated tap water.)

Stay away from high altitudes. Traveling to destinations above 5,000 feet where the air is "thin" may only cause you more distress. Check with your doctor.

Drink plenty of liquids. To counteract the dry air in an airplane cabin or air-conditioned room, drink plenty of water or juice. This will keep the mucous membranes in your nose and throat from drying.

Now that you're ready to tackle the toughest problems you're likely to encounter while traveling, let's move on to some smaller—but delightfully so—challenges: your grandchildren.

IN SUMMARY...

☑ Before you commit to a travel itinerary, get your doctor's blessing on your destination and planned activities.

☑ Have a plan for getting your medications through customs, adjusting your dosing schedule to a new time zone and replacing your prescription drugs in case they are lost or stolen.

☑ Schedule chemotherapy or dialysis treatments at another treatment center well in advance of travel. Your doctor can help you locate appropriate resources near your destination for easy access in case of an emergency.

☑ Make sure your medical insurance will cover treatments and emergencies, especially if you plan to travel outside the United States.

☑ Subscribe to Medic Alert and carry important medical information with you, so you'll be properly cared for if you are unconscious or can't speak for yourself.

☑ Make sure you have the proper immunizations before you depart.

☑ Know your limits. Stress and anxiety may trigger health problems. At the first sign of fatigue or anxiety, slow down.

☑ Know what to do in the event of a heart attack.

☑ Stay away from high-altitude destinations if you have cardiovascular or respiratory ailments.

☑ If you're traveling to a hot, humid climate, plan to take an air-conditioned siesta from 11 a.m. to 3 p.m.

☑ Don't fly if you've had a stroke within the previous two weeks or a heart attack within the previous four weeks.

☑ U-100 insulin is not available in some countries. Carry twice as much insulin as you'll need as well as a written prescription for syringes.

☑ Never carry pre-filled syringes, and properly store the insulin you carry. Never use insulin if clumps have formed or if it has become discolored.

☑ Carry glucose gels, tablets, or another sugar source in case of an insulin reaction.

☑ If you have kidney disease don't travel far from a hospital with a hemodialysis unit. A list of worldwide dialysis facilities is available from *Dialysis and Transplantation Magazine* (818-782-7328).

☑ Cold, hot and dry air as well as local allergens can precipitate a range of respiratory conditions. Make sure you have an adequate supply of oxygen and inhalers.

Chapter 13

Traveling with your grandchildren

One of the great joys of being a grandparent is being able to spend quality time getting to know your grandchildren. Travel provides a wonderful opportunity. So whether you plan a fun-filled day at the local amusement park or a week-long educational tour of the nation's capital, here are some guidelines for protecting their health—and your sanity—en route.

Consult your children. You remember what it was like being a parent. Each child has his or her own schedule, anxieties, favorite toys. Your children will help get you started on the right foot with your grandchildren.

Involve your grandchildren. Let young children carry their own suitcase or backpack. Pack a Polaroid camera and help them take photos they can see in minutes. Shop together for gifts and souvenirs of the trip. Buy postcards they can mail back home.

If your grandchildren are a bit older, ask them what sites they especially want to see. Send them books about the history of the places you plan to visit.

Don't plan too much for one day. Young children are easily distracted and may be used to regular naps.

Maintain a "normal" routine. Plan to drive during the time children will be sleeping or napping. If they insist on staying awake, pull out Auto Bingo or coloring books to keep them occupied during long stretches of driving. You can wind a wound-up child with quiet activities, such as reading.

How to calm a frightened child

Some children will find a new environment frightening at first. Here are some tips for easing their fears:

♦ Familiarize children with travel plans ahead of time. Send them a map with the route marked and brochures or picture books before you leave. Then remind them of these sights while you're traveling.

♦ Take mini-trips to the airport. As soon as a child feels comfortable in strange surroundings, anxiety will turn to excitement.

♦ Pack favorite toys, books and games to hold the attention of children under 4 years.

♦ For older children (4 to 9 years), buy new puzzles, cartoon books and travel-size games and toys especially for the trip.

♦ Comfort a child with a favorite stuffed animal, blanket, story book or even bath toy or towel. These items can work wonders when children have trouble falling asleep in a strange bed.

♦ Pack plenty of snacks, such as raisins, crackers, cereal and boxed juices.

♦ Take frequent rest stops and plan to travel short distances each day if you're driving.

How to keep children healthy—and happy

Much of the information contained in this book is as applicable for children as it is for senior travelers. Here are a few exceptions.

Protect each child from the sun with a hat and a sunscreen with an SPF of at least 15. A child's skin is more sensitive to the sun than an adult's. Be sure to reapply sunscreen every hour or two—more often if children are swimming.

Encourage children to drink a lot of water and juice while traveling. Carry bottled water, since many children are sensitive to changes in water, even when traveling within the United States.

If a child becomes dehydrated after diarrhea, give him or her Pedialyte to replace lost sodium and potassium. If Pedialyte isn't available, add one-half teaspoon of sugar and a pinch of salt to fruit juice as a substitute.

Reduce the discomfort of taking off and landing for babies by giving them a pacifier or bottle. Encourage older children to chew gum or suck on hard candy. Swallowing more will clear their ears.

Take prescription medications as well as the telephone number of a pediatrician.

Next we're off to another popular travel alternative for seniors—mixing business (travel) with a pleasure excursion.

IN SUMMARY....

☑ Your own children are the best source of important information about your grandchildren's schedule, anxieties and favorite toys. Consult them before you plan a trip.

☑ Involve children in planning the trip.

☑ Young children are easily distracted and used to regular naps, so don't plan to do too much in one day.

☑ Take mini-trips to the airport to ease a child's anxiety about traveling.

☑ Pack familiar toys, books, games and snacks to comfort and occupy your grandchildren.

☑ A child's skin is more sensitive to the sun. Pack a hat and frequently apply sunscreen with an SPF of 15.

☑ Children can be especially sensitive to changes in water, even when traveling within the United States. Carry bottled water. If a child becomes dehydrated after a bout with diarrhea, give him or her Pedialyte or add one-half teaspoon of sugar and a pinch of salt to fruit juice to replace lost sodium and potassium.

☑ On flights, babies should be given a pacifier or bottle during take-off and landing. Older children can chew gum or suck on hard candy.

☑ Along with prescription medications, take the telephone number of your grandchildren's pediatrician.

Chapter 14

Mixing business with pleasure

If you already travel regularly for business or as a retired consultant or speaker, why not invite you spouse along—to check out a future retirement spot or celebrate your 40th anniversary in an exotic destination? Even if you'll be on your own, there may never be a better time to spend a few free days enjoying an exciting new destination.

How to balance work and play

Here are some tips for balancing the stress of business travel with the enjoyment of a pleasure trip.

Plan ahead for jet lag. If you'll be flying across several time zones, plan ahead to reduce the effects of jet lag. You'll find the detailed information you need in Chapter 3.

Be prepared. If you plan to save time for pleasure travel, plan to do as much work as you can before you leave. Save the rest for when you return. You want to get out to see the sights, not spend the day on the phone in your room.

Don't overindulge. It may be tempting to overeat or drink when someone else is picking up the tab. But you need to be in peak condition for important meetings or presentations. Opt for moderation.

And if you're sampling new cuisine in a foreign country, review the precautions in Chapter 5.

Relax. Whether at work or play, make use of the hotel or cruise ship's health club, pool, sauna and whirlpools. Schedule a massage. Take a stroll along the beach or grounds. Dine in that rooftop restaurant with the incredible 360-degree view.

Bring your own relaxation. Maybe now is the time for that novel you haven't had time to read or to spend as much time as you want getting just the right five shots of a famous landmark.

Be adventurous. Even if you're alone, don't be shy about tagging along on a city tour or stopping into the fabulous restaurant the concierge suggested. Check out special events such as plays and sporting events. Try a new activity, such a snorkeling.

Stay in touch. Provide family members with your complete travel schedule, and check in regularly.

Carry this book along. I think you'll find it an invaluable companion you can consult again and again throughout your travels.

Bon voyage.

Organizations serving the senior traveler

Where to file a complaint

American Society of Travel Agents (ASTA). You can file a complaint about a travel agency or check an agency's complaint record, by calling 703-739-2782, or writing:

American Society of Travel
    Agents
Consumer Affairs
1101 King Street
Alexandria, VA 22314

Note: ASTA's power can be limited in some cases, so your first choice should be to contact your local Better Business Bureau.

U.S. Department of Transportation. Contact this agency to file a formal complaint against an airline if you feel you haven't received a satisfactory response from the airline. Send your written complaint to:

U.S. Department of
    Transportation
Office of Consumer Affairs
I-25, 400 7th Street SW
Washington, DC 20590
202-366-2220

Where to get up-to-date information

Cruise Ship Sanitation Survey. Twice a year, the U.S. Centers for Disease Control rates all cruise ships that dock at U.S. ports on food preparation and holding, water quality, storage and repair procedures, and general cleanliness. You can get a free copy of this report by writing to:

The Vessel Sanitation Program
Center for Environmental Health
1015 N. American Way
Room 107
Miami, FL 33132

International Association for Medical Assistance to Travelers (IAMAT). This organization is an excellent resource for comprehensive information about health risks around the world, a listing of English-speaking doctors practicing overseas and climate charts specific for your destination. To request this information, write:

IAMAT, 417 Center Street
Lewiston, NY 14092
716-754-4883

U.S. Centers for Disease Control. This federal bureau provides a 24-hour hotline with health-related information for travelers. Call 404-332-4559 from a touch-tone phone and follow the easy-to-understand instructions. The information is up-to-date and essential for anyone traveling outside the U.S.

U.S. State Department. Call 202-647-5225 anytime for a recorded list of travel advisories that may affect the safety of U.S. travelers throughout the world. If you wish to speak to an operator, call 202-647-5226 during normal business hours.

Where to get the best traveler's insurance

Many travel agencies and tour operators sell travel insurance. The problem is that some travel agencies choose a travel insurance company based on what level of commission the travel agency receives in return.

To get the best policy, call several travel insurance companies and compare rates and coverage. The companies listed below provide both medical and trip insurance.

Access America
800-284-8300

American Express Travel Protection Plan
800-234-0375

Carefree Travel Insurance
800-323-3149

CSA Inc.
800-626-1031

International SOS Assistance
800-523-8930

Travel Assistance International
800-821-2828

Travel Assure (Mutual of Omaha)
800-228-9792

Travel Guard International
800-826-1300

Travel Insurance Pak (Travelers Insurance)
800-243-3174

Where to report lost or stolen traveler's checks

If you're traveling outside the U.S., ask for the telephone number(s) of foreign offices close to your specific destination overseas.

American Express
Continental U.S. 800-221-7282
Alaska and Hawaii
800-221-7280

Bank of America
Continental U.S. 800-227-3460
Outside U.S. (call collect)
415-624-5400

Citicorp 800-525-9040

MasterCard
U.S. 800-826-2181
Outside U.S. (call collect)
212-974-5696

Visa
U.S. 800-336-8472
Outside U.S. 800-227-6811

Thomas Cook
U.S. 800-223-7373
Outside U.S. (call collect) 609-987-7300

Diners Club
U.S. (except Colorado)
800-525-9040
Colorado only 800-332-9340

Discover Card 800-347-2683

Directory of diseases

African Sleeping Sickness

Caused by a microscopic parasite.

> **How you get it:** Transmitted by the tsetse fly, most prevalent in Africa around the equator.
>
> **Symptoms:** Fever, headache and fatigue, followed by skin rash, swelling and central nervous system collapse.
>
> **Prognosis:** May be fatal, unless treated with pharmaceuticals.

Amebiasis

Caused by a protozoa.

> **How you get it:** Through contaminated food and water in underdeveloped countries and areas with poor sanitation.
>
> **Symptoms:** Severe diarrhea.
>
> **Prognosis:** May affect major organs, causing death unless treated with pharmaceuticals.

Bartonellosis

Caused by a bacteria.

> **How you get it:** Sand fly bite in the mountains of Peru, Ecuador and Colombia.
>
> **Symptoms:** Fever, bone and/or joint, and muscle pain.
>
> **Prognosis:** Treated with pharmaceuticals.

Cholera

Caused by a bacteria.

> **How you get it:** Contaminated food and water in Africa and Asia.
>
> **Symptoms:** Diarrhea, stomach cramps, dehydration, nausea and vomiting.
>
> **Prognosis:** May be fatal, unless treated with pharmaceuticals and re-hydration.

Colorado Tick Fever

Caused by a virus.

How you get it: Transmitted by the bite of the wood tick in western U.S. and Canada.

Symptoms: Intense muscle aches in the back and legs, fever, chills, headache, stomach pain, meningitis and, in some cases, a rash.

Prognosis: Most people recover in about 3-4 weeks.

Diphtheria

Caused by a bacteria.

How you get it: Prevalent in the temperate zone and in non-immunized populations.

Symptoms: Swelling of the throat.

Prognosis: May be fatal unless treated with antitoxin.

Encephalitis

Caused by a virus.

How you get it: Infected mosquitoes and ticks virtually anywhere.

Symptoms: Flu-like symptoms.

Prognosis: May be fatal unless treated with pharmaceuticals and supportive therapy.

Giardiasis

Caused by a protozoa.

How you get it: Contaminated food and water in underdeveloped countries and countries with poor sanitation.

Symptoms: Severe diarrhea and cramps, gas, nausea and vomiting.

Prognosis: Fatal if severe dehydration occurs from the diarrhea. Treat with pharmaceuticals.

Hepatitis

Caused by a virus.

How you get it: Direct contact, contaminated food and water in underdeveloped countries with poor sanitation.

Symptoms: Fatigue, nausea, vomiting, muscle and joint pain, headache. Ultimately jaundice and liver pain.

Prognosis: May be fatal unless supportive care is received. A vaccine can prevent the disease.

Leprosy

Caused by a bacteria.

How you get it: Unknown. It is most prevalent in the tropics and India but new cases are rare.

Symptoms: Skin lesions and sores.

Prognosis: Treated with pharmaceuticals.

Lyme Disease
Caused by a bacteria.

How you get it: Tick bite during the summer in wooded areas.

Symptoms: A bulls eye-like rash around the site of the bite, accompanied with flu-like symptoms.

Prognosis: Treated with pharmaceuticals.

Malaria
Caused by a parasite.

How you get it: Infected Anopheles mosquito in most tropical regions of the world and Africa. (For a complete list of countries, see Chapter 10.)

Symptoms: Fever, chills, flu-like symptoms.

Prognosis: More than 300 million cases are reported annually, with approximately 1 million deaths occurring. Treat with pharmaceuticals. Consult with your doctor about starting malaria prophylaxis before departing to any foreign country.

Measles
Caused by a virus.

How you get it: It is transmitted by direct contact with airborne droplets from an infected nose or mouth.

Symptoms: Fatigue, fever, runny nose, cough and eventually a rash.

Prognosis: There is no treatment except for preventive vaccines. The disease itself usually goes away, but severe secondary infections may occur.

Meningitis
Caused by a bacteria.

How you get it: Direct contact with airborne droplets from an infected nose or mouth in Africa, especially during the dry season.

Symptoms: The disease causes an inflammation of the lining of the brain with flu-like symptoms and sometimes a rash.

Prognosis: Fatal unless treated with pharmaceuticals.

Puffer Fish Poisoning
Caused by the toxin in the puffer fish.

How you get it: Eating puffer fish during its reproductive season. The fish is considered a delicacy in the Far East. It should only be eaten in the winter and only in licensed restaurants.

Symptoms: Excessive sweating and salivation followed by low blood pressure, numbness and difficulty in breathing.

Prognosis: As many as 50 percent of those poisoned die without supportive therapy.

Rabies

Caused by a virus.

How you get it: Bite of an infected animal anywhere. About 15,000 cases are reported worldwide annually.

Symptoms: The disease affects the central nervous system. Symptoms include fever, headache, chills, fatigue, sore throat, muscle aches and cough.

Prognosis: Fatal if not treated. Treat with a series of shots if the animal can't be found to check for rabies.

Rocky Mountain Spotted Fever

Caused by a bacteria.

How you get it: Bite of an infected tick in the western hemisphere.

Symptoms: Longlasting fever, chills, headaches and a rash on the arms and legs.

Prognosis: Fatal unless treated with pharmaceuticals.

Salmonellosis

Caused by a bacteria.

How you get it: Contaminated food and water in underdeveloped countries and countries with poor sanitation.

Symptoms: Stomach pain, nausea, vomiting, diarrhea and fever.

Prognosis: Rarely fatal. Only treatment is supportive therapy and rehydration. It can be prevented by eating only well-cooked foods.

Schistosomiasis

Caused by a parasitic flat worm.

How you get it: Bathing in freshwater lakes and rivers in Brazil, Surinam, Venezuela, Africa, China, Philippines and parts of the Caribbean.

Symptoms: Itchy rash, fatigue, loss of appetite, fever and bloody, painful or frequent urination.

Prognosis: Fatal unless treated with pharmaceuticals.

Trachoma

Caused by a virus-like organism.

How you get it: Direct contact with hand, towels, etc. Also from flies in Africa, the Middle East and parts of Asia.

Symptoms: Inflamed eyelids, and turned in eyelashes that scratch and damage the eye.

Prognosis: It affects over 380 million people annually and causes over 190 million cases of blindness each year. Treat with pharmaceuticals.

Trichinosis
Caused by a worm.

How you get it: Eating meat that is undercooked, usually pork. It is found worldwide especially in Europe and North America.

Symptoms: Stomach pain, diarrhea, fever, nausea and fatigue.

Prognosis: Usually not fatal if treated with pharmaceuticals. Prevent this disease by eating only well-cooked or smoked meats.

Tuberculosis
Caused by a bacteria.

How you get it: Airborne droplets from infected people or through unpasteurized milk or milk products. It is found throughout the world and is again becoming more prevalent.

Symptoms: Persistent cough, fever and weight loss.

Prognosis: May be fatal unless treated with pharmaceuticals.

Typhoid Fever
Caused by a bacteria.

How you get it: Contaminated food and water in Africa, Asia and Central and South America.

Symptoms: Headaches, fever, stomach pain, fatigue and possible rash.

Prognosis: Can be fatal unless treated with pharmaceuticals.

Typhus Fever
Caused by a bacteria-like organism.

How you get it: Bites from infected fleas, lice, mites and ticks in mountain regions of Mexico, Africa, Asia, Central and South America, Eastern Europe and Northern Australia.

Symptoms: Fever, rash, headache and muscle pain.

Prognosis: May be fatal in as few as two weeks if not treated with pharmaceuticals.

Yellow Fever
Caused by a virus.

How you get it: Bite of an infected mosquito in Africa, Central and South America.

Symptoms: "Black vomit," fever, muscle pain, nausea, jaundice, no urine output and hemorrhaging.

Prognosis: May be fatal unless treated with supportive therapy. There is a vaccine available. Consult your doctor before traveling to any high-risk area.

Important reservation numbers

Airlines

Aeromexico	(800) 237-6639
Air Afrique	(800) 456-9192
Air Canada	(800) 776-3000
Alitalia	(800) 223-5730
America West	(800) 235-9292
American	(800) 433-7300
British Airways	(800) 247-9297
Continental	(800) 525-0280
Delta	(800) 221-1212
Iberia of Spain	(800) 772-4642
Japan	(800) 525-3663
KLM Royal Dutch	(800) 374-8866
Thrifty	(800) 367-2277
Lufthansa	(800) 645-3880
Midwest Express	(800) 452-2022
Northwest	(800) 225-2525
Phillipine	(800) 435-9725
Quantas	(800) 227-4500
Scandinavian	(800) 221-2350
Skyway	(800) 452-2022
Southwest	(800) 435-9792
Swissair	(800) 221-4750
TWA	(800) 221-2000
United	(800) 241-6522
USAir	(800) 428-4322
Varig Brazilian	(800) 468-2744

Car rental companies

Alamo	(800) 327-9633
Avis	(800) 331-1212
Budget	(800) 527-0700
Connex	(800) 333-3949
Dollar	(800) 800-4000
Enterprise	(800) 325-8007
Hertz	(800) 654-3131
Holiday	(800) 422-7737
General	(800) 327-7607
National	(800) 227-7368
Payless	(800) 237-2804
Thrifty	(800) 367-2277

Hotels and motels

Aston	(800) 922-7866
Best Western	(800) 528-1234
Budgetel Inn	(800) 428-3438
Colony	(800) 777-1700
Courtyard By Marriott	(800) 321-2211
Days Inn	(800) 325-2525
Embassy Suites	(800) 362-2779
Fairfield Inn	(800) 228-2800
Guest Quarters Suites	(800) 424-2900
Hampton Inn	(800) 426-7866
Hilton	(800) 445-8667
Holiday Inn	(800) 465-4329
Howard Johnson	(800) 654-2000
Hyatt	(800) 228-3360
La Quinta	(800) 531-5900
Marriott	(800) 228-9290
Quality Inns	(800) 221-2222
Ramada	(800) 722-9467
Red Roof Inns	(800) 843-7663
Shoney's Inns	(800) 222-2222
Signature Inns	(800) 822-5252
Stouffer	(800) 468-3571
Travelodge	(800) 255-3050
Westin	(800) 228-3000
Woodfin Suites	(800) 237-8811

Tourism bureaus

Here's how to reach the tourism bureaus in each of the 50 states and District of Columbia to obtain information on sites and attractions.

Alabama	800-252-2262
Alaska	907-465-2010
Arizona	800-842-8257
Arkansas	800-628-8725
California	800-862-2543
Colorado	800-608-4748
Connecticut	800-282-6863
Delaware	800-441-8846
District of Columbia	202-789-7000
Florida	904-487-1462
Georgia	800-847-4842
Hawaii	808-923-1811
Idaho	800-635-7820
Illinois	800-223-0121
Indiana	800-289-6646
Iowa	800-345-4692
Kansas	800-252-6727
Kentucky	800-225-8747
Louisiana	800-334-8626
Maine	800-533-9595
Maryland	800-543-1036
Massachusetts	800-447-6277
Michigan	800-543-2937
Minnesota	800-657-3700
Mississippi	800-927-6378
Missouri	800-877-1234

Montana	800-541-1447	Rhode Island	800-556-2484
Nebraska	800-228-4307	South Carolina	800-346-3634
Nevada	800-638-2328	South Dakota	800-732-5682
New Hampshire	603-271-2343	Tennessee	800-847-4886
New Jersey	800-537-7397	Texas	800-888-8839
New Mexico	800-545-2040	Utah	800-200-1160
New York	800-225-5697	Vermont	800-837-6668
North Carolina	800-847-4862	Virginia	800-847-4882
North Dakota	800-435-5663	Washington	800-544-1800
Ohio	800-282-5393	West Virginia	800-225-5982
Oklahoma	800-652-6552	Wisconsin	800-432-8747
Oregon	800-547-7842	Wyoming	800-225-5996
Pennsylvania	800-847-4872		

Directory of travel health care consultants

The following is a list of physicians who offer clinical consulta-tive service in tropical medicine, medical parasitology and traveler's health.

The list does not include all physicians who provide travel health care services and does not imply endorsement or verification of credentials or expertise of those listed.

Alabama

Freedman, David O., MD
University of Alabama at
    Birmingham
Traveler's Health Clinic
Division of Geographic Medicine
1025 18th St. S., Rm. 240
Birmingham, AL 35205

Appointments: 205-934-4000
Acute illnesses:205-934-1630
205-934-3411 (evenings)
Pretravel medical consultation; immunizations, consultation; parasitology lab.

Arizona

Kuberski, Tim, MD
5757 W. Thunderbird Rd., Ste. W212
Glendale, AZ 85306
602-439-0274
Hours: 24; Tropical medicine and infectious diseases.

Fanning, Lee, W., MD, FACP
Scottsdale Medical Clinic
3501 N. Scottsdale Rd., Ste. 300
Scottsdale, AZ 85251
602-949-2080
Travel health information / immunizations. Expert in infectious diseases.

Cordes, D. H., MD
Travelers' Clinic
University of Arizona
Tucson, AZ 85724
602-626-7900
Medical evaluations; counseling; prescriptions; immunizations.

Peate, Wayne F., MD, M.P.H.
Corporate Medical Ctr.
2545 E. Adams St.
Tucson, AZ 85716
601-881-0050

Hours: Mon.-Fri., 8 a.m.-5 p.m.
Clinical tropical medicine including
immunizations and medications.

California

Palmer, Philip E. S., FRCP, FRCR
Dept. of Radiology
University of California at Davis
Davis, CA 95616
916-752-7057

Hours: 24; Tropical radiology.

Beal, Charles, MD, President
International Health Services
1898 Bay Rd.
East Palo Alto, CA 94303
415-325-7364
415-476-5787

Tropical medicine, infectious diseases
and travelers' clinic
Hours: travelers' clinic, daily
9 a.m.-5 p.m. Tropical medicine
clinic: Wed. 1-5 p.m. Immunizations.

Baker, Lawrence A., DO
Coastal Medical Centre
    Travelers' Clinic
317 North El Camino Real, Suite 506
Encinitas, CA 92024
619-943-7262

Hours: Mon.-Fri. 9 a.m.-5 p.m.
All immunizations.

Panosian, Claire B., MD, Director
UCLA Travelers' and Tropical
    Medicine Clinic
UCLA Medical Center
10833 LeConte Ave.
Los Angeles, CA 90024
310-206-7663

Hours: Tue. 1-5 p.m., Fri. 9 a.m.-
12:30 p.m. Standard travel counsel;
immunization; post-travel diagnostic
evaluation and treatment.

Frierson, J. Gordon, MD, DTM&H
Tropical Medicine-Infectious Disease
    Clinic and Travelers' Clinic
University of California
    San Francisco
350 Parnassus St.
San Francisco, CA 94143
415-476-5787

Hours: Clinics, Wed. 8 a.m.-noon; Of-
fice, by appointment. Immunizations.

Stein, Madlyn, MD, M.P.H.
350-30th St., Ste. 134
    (The Travel Doctor)
Oakland, CA 94609
510-763-5336

Hours by appointment. Consultation
on travelers' health and tropical
medicine. All immunizations.

Barrett-Connor, Elizabeth, MD,
  Director
Rosen, David, MD, Co-Director
UCSD Medical Center
Family Medicine Clinic
225 W. Dickinson
San Diego, CA 92103
619-543-5787

Hours: Tue. 1-4 p.m.
Immunizations; evaluation of trav-
eler-related problems; University
hospital diagnostic lab.

Kovner, Victor L., MD, FACP
Travelers' Immunization Center
12311 Ventura Blvd.
Studio City, CA 91604
818-762-1167

Hours: Mon.-Fri. 9 a.m.-5 p.m. by
appointment. Immunizations; health
education for tropics; infectious dis-
eases consultation; lab.

Connecticut

Hill, David R., MD
International Travelers' Medical
  Service
University of Connecticut Health
  Center
Farmington, CT 06030-3212
203-679-4225 or 4700

Hours: Wed. 9 a.m.-12:30 p.m. Or by
appointment.
Full pre- and post-travel medical
care; all immunizations.

Barry, Michele, MD, Co-Director
Tropical Medicine and International
  Travelers' Clinic
Yale University School of Medicine
20 York St.
New Haven, CT 06504
203-785-2476/after 5 p.m. 785-2471

Hours: 24. Clinic weekly (Fri. p.m.)
Immunizations; computer-generated
analysis of health and vaccination
requirements; hepatitis screening;
viral and parasitic lab services; infec-
tious diseases and tropical medicine
consultation.

Dardick, Kenneth R., MD, FACP,
  DTM&H
Connecticut Travel Medicine
Mansfield Professional Park
Storrs, CT 06268
203-487-0002, Fax: 203-429-1663

Hours: Mon.-Thur. 8 a.m.-9 p.m.;
Fri. 8 a.m.-5 p.m.; Sat. 8 a.m.-noon.
Pre-travel consultation; immuniza-
tions; post-travel diagnosis and
treatment.

District of Columbia

Grigsby, Margaret E., MD, FACP,
  DTMH (London)
Howard University Hospital
2041 Georgia Ave. NW
Washington, DC 20060
202-865-1901, Fax: 202-745-3731

Hours: Mon.-Fri. 9 a.m.-5 p.m.
Tropical medicine; infectious diseases;
travelers' health; all immunizations.

Mody, Vinod R., Dr. FRCP, DTM&H
Chief Geographic Medicine
Howard University Hospital
2041 Georgia Ave. NW
Washington, DC 20060
202-745-6641

*Hours by appointment. International
travel; advised immunizations; lab.*

Wolfe, Martin S., MD
Travelers' Medical Service
2141 K St. NW, Rm. 408
Washington, DC 20037
202-466-8109

*Hours: Mon-Fri 9 a.m.-5 p.m.
by appointment. Immunizations;
tropical medicine consultations.*

Florida

Reifsnyder, David N., MD
901 N. Hercules Ave., Ste. C
Clearwater, FL 34625
813-446-3515

*Hours: 9 a.m.-3 p.m., Mon., Tue.,
Thur., Fri. (by appointment). Exams;
lab tests; immunizations at nearby
health department.*

Kammerer, William S., MD
Mayo Clinic
4500 San Pablo Rd.
Jacksonville, FL 32224
904-223-2497

*Hours: Mon.-Fri. 8 a.m.-5 p.m.
All immunizations; clinical problems
in returning travelers; chronically ill*

*travelers; all diagnostic testing
available.*

MacLeod, Caroline, MD, MPH & TM
Tropical Medicine and Travelers'
    Clinic
3741 Le Jeune Rd. SW
Miami, FL 33146
305-663-9666
Fax: 305-663-9671

*Hours: Mon.-Sat. 9 a.m.-4 p.m.
Complete travel services; immunizations and counseling; evaluation of
tropical diseases.*

Whiteside, Mark E., MD
Institute of Tropical Medicine
Partner: Dr. Caroline L. MacLeod
1780 NE 168th St.
North Miami Beach, FL 33162
305-947-1722

*Hours: Mon.-Fri. 9 a.m.-5 p.m.
Complete travel services; immunizations and counseling; evaluation of
tropical diseases.*

Georgia

Blumenthal, Daniel S., MD, MPH
Morehouse Family Practice Center
501 Fairburn Rd. SW
Atlanta, GA 30331
404-752-1624

*Hours: Mon.-Fri. 9 a.m.-5 p.m.
Immunizations given, but not for yellow fever.*

Kozarsky, Phyllis E., MD
Travel Well International Travelers'
    Medical Clinic
The Emory Clinic/Crawford Long
    Hospital of Emory University
20 Linden Ave., NE, Ste. 101-G
Atlanta, GA 30365
404-686-8114

Hours by appointment, 24 hour emergency coverage. Pre-travel evaluation and counseling; care of returning travelers; all recommended and required immunizations; complete lab.

Hawaii

Pien, Francis D., MD
Straub Clinic & Hospital, Inc.
888 South King St.
Honolulu, HI 96813
808-523-2311

Diagnosis, treatment; vaccinations.

Iowa

Nettleman, Mary, MD
Director, Travel and Tropical
    Medicine Clinic, University of
    Iowa Hospitals and Clinics
Iowa City, IA 52242
319-356-4254

Hours by appointment. Full clinical and lab services; all immunizations.

Kansas

Rumans, Larry W., MD
631 Horne, Suite 420
Topeka, KS 66606
913-234-8405

Hours: Mon.-Fri. 8 a.m.-5 p.m. Infectious diseases; medical microbiology and tropical medicine; immunizations given (no yellow fever).

Louisiana

Krotoski, WA, MD, Ph.D., MPH
Tropical Medicine Consultation
11620 Rue de Tonti
Baton Rouge, LA 70810
504-769-7496

Hours: Evenings and weekends. Consultations.

Hoadley, Deborah, MD, MPH & TM
Tulane Travel and Tropical Medicine
    Clinic
Tulane Medical Center
1415 Tulane Ave.
New Orleans, LA 70112
504-588-5580

Hours: Tropical medicine, Thur. 9 a.m.-noon. Pre-travel counseling on a walk-in basis: Mon.-Fri. 8 a.m.-5 p.m. Pre-travel prophylaxis and evaluation of returning travelers, including children; all immunizations.

Maine

Smith, Robert P., MD
Spurwink Internal Medicine Assoc.
155 Spurwink Ave.
Cape Elizabeth, ME 04107
207-767-2174

Hours: Every day. Consultation on infectious diseases with prospective and returning travelers; immunizations (not yellow fever).

Maryland

Edelman, Robert, MD
Travelers' Health Service
University of Maryland Medical
     Group
University of Maryland Hospital
Baltimore, MD 21201
301-328-5196

Hours: Wed. 1-4 p.m. All care for pre- and post-travel; diagnosis and treatment of endemic diseases; immunizations; lab tests.

Sack, R. Bradley, MD
Johns Hopkins International
     Medical Services
550 N. Broadway, Rm. 107
Baltimore, MD 21205
301-955-6931

Hours: 8:30 a.m.-5 p.m. daily Pre-travel and post-travel consultations; immunizations; lab.

Pesce, Carlo, MD
National Institutes of Health
Building 10, Room 2N212
Bethesda, MD 20892
301-496-2441

Hours: Mon.-Fri. 9 a.m.-5 p.m. Tropical pathology; consultations on slides and histological specimens from the tropics.

Scheibel, Leonard William, MD
F. Edward Herbert School of Medicine
Division of Tropical Public Health
4301 Jones Bridge Rd.
Bethesda, MD 20814-4799
202-295-3730

Hours: Mon.-Fri. 9 a.m.-5 p.m. Consultation.

Massachusetts

Felsenstein, Donna, MD
Travelers' Advice and Immunization
     Center
Massachusetts General Hospital
Wang ACC 037
Boston, MA 02114
617-726-3906

Hours: Travelers' advice and immunizations: Mon.-Fri. 8:30 a.m.- 12:30 p.m., Mon. and Wed. 1-4 p.m. by appointment. Consultation for patients with tropical and/or parasitic diseases.

Maguire, James H., MD
Brigham & Womens Hospital
75 Francis St.
Boston, MA 02115
617-732-6801

Hours by appointment. Emergencies through page. Clinical care of patients with infectious diseases and parasitic diseases.

Wilson, Mary E., MD
Mount Auburn Hospital
Division of Infectious Diseases
330 Mt. Auburn St.
Cambridge, MA 02238
617-499-5026 or 617-499-5055

Hours: Mon.-Fri. 9 a.m.-5 p.m., call for appointment. Evaluation of patients with suspected infections after travel or residence in tropical country; immunizations.

Michigan

Fisher, Evelyn J., MD
Travel Health Clinic
Division of Infectious Diseases
Henry Ford Hospital
2799 West Grant Blvd.
Detroit, MI 48202
313-876-2556
(after hours: 313-876-2600)

Hours: Mon.-Fri. 9 a.m.-5 p.m. Pre- and post-travel counseling; tropical medicine consultation.

Haas, Erwin J., MD
2150 East Beltline, SE
Grand Rapids, MI 49546
616-942-1271 or 616-942-7674

Consultation; tropical and travelers' medicine.

Band, Jeffrey D., MD, Director
InterHealth R—Health Care for
    International Travelers
William Beaumont Hospital
Medical Office Building, Ste. 707
3535 West Thirteen Mile Rd.
Royal Oak, MI 48072
313-288-2736

Hours: Mon-Fri 8:30 a.m.-5 p.m. by appointment. Pre-travel medical evaluations and counseling; all immunizations; post-travel screening and evaluations.

Missouri

Weil, Gary J., MD
Infectious Diseases Division
Jewish Hospital at Washington
    University Medical Center
216 South Kings Highway
St. Louis, MO 63110
314-454-7782

Hours: Call for appointment. By physician referral. Diagnostic lab.

Nevada

Cross, Karen L., MD
International Travel and
    Immunization Clinic, Chtd.
1641 East Flamingo, Ste. 10
Las Vegas, NV 89119
702-733-7468

Hours: Mon. 4-8 p.m. Pre-travel consultation; immunizations.

New Jersey

Gluckman, Stephen J., MD
Cooper Hospital/University Medical
    Center
3 Cooper Plaza, Ste. 215
Camden, NJ 08103
609-342-2439

*Hours: Mon.-Fri. 8 a.m.-5 p.m.
Immunizations; infectious diseases.*

New York

Rush, Thomas J., MD
Infectious Diseases & Travel Health
141 North State Rd.
Briarcliff Manor, NY 10510
914-762-2276

Hours: Thur. 1-5 p.m., or by appointment. Immunizations.

Tanowitz, Herbert MD
Albert Einstein College of Medicine
1300 Morris Park Ave.
Bronx, NY 10461
212-430-2059

*Hours: Mon.-Fri. 9 a.m.-5 p.m. by
appointment. Immunizations;*

*tropical medicine and parasitology
consultation; complete parasitology
lab including immunologic tests for
parasites.*

Lee, Richard V., MD
Department of Medicine
Childrens Hospital of Buffalo
219 Bryant St.
Buffalo, NY 14222
716-878-7751

All immunizations.

Cunha, Burke A., MD
Infectious Disease International
    Travelers' Center
Winthrop-University Hospital
259 First St.
Mineola, L.I., NY 11501
516-663-2505

Hours by appointment.

Connor, Bradley A., MD
Travel Health Services
50 East 69th St.
New York, NY 10021
212-734-3000 or 212-570-4000

*Hours: 24 hour coverage; appointments. Mon.-Fri. 8:30 a.m.-5 p.m.,
Tue. 5-7:30 p.m. Comprehensive
health care for the international traveler; pre-travel medical evaluations
and counseling; immunizations; post-travel follow-up.*

Giordano, Michael F., MD
New York Hospital/Cornell Medical
    Center
Helmsley Tower, Rm. 360
New York, NY 10021
212-746-2397

Hours: Mon.-Fri. 8 a.m.-5 p.m., eve-
nings by special appointment. On call
24 hours. All immunizations; post-
travel evaluations; tropical medicine
and infectious diseases consultations.

Hoskins, Donald W., MD
311 East 79th St.
New York, NY 10021
212-879-6004

Hours: Mon.-Fri. by appointment.
Tropical medicine; travelers' health
and parasitology; all immunizations
(not yellow fever).

Most, Harry, MD
New York University Medical Center
341 E. 25 St., Rm. 105
New York, NY 10010
212-340-6764

Hours by appointment. Immuniza-
tion; consultations; full lab.

Feinstein, Stuart, MD
7 Fox St.
Poughkeepsie, NY 12601
914-471-0232

Hours by appointment. Comprehen-
sive international travel counseling;
treatment of infectious diseases and
parasitic diseases; immunizations.

North Carolina

Herrington, Deidre, MD
International Travel Clinic
Section on Infectious Diseases
Bowman Grey School of Medicine
Wake Forest University
Winston-Salem, NC 27103
919-748-4516

Hours: Mon. 1-5 p.m. All care for pre-
and post-travel diagnosis; treatment
of endemic diseases; all immuniza-
tions; lab tests.

Ohio

Ostendorf, Richard, MD, FACEP
Prompt Care
17747 Chillicothe
Chagrin Falls, OH 44022
216-543-8855

Open daily. Appointments made at
patient's convenience. Immunizations
for travel; pre-travel includes com-
puterized information on itinerary.

Pennsylvania

Schenfield, Louis A., MD, FACP
1111 Franklin St.
Johnstown, PA 15905
814-539-3666

Hours: Mon.-Fri.9 a.m.-4 p.m. (by
appointment). Full pre- and post-
travel medical care; all immunizations;
lab at hospital.

Sfedu, Emil P., MD
Executive Health Services, Inc.
716 North 24th St.
Philadelphia, PA 19130
215-235-3000

*Hours: Mon.-Thur. 9 a.m.-7:30 p.m.,
Fri. 9 a.m.-6 p.m., Sat. 10 a.m.-2 p.m.
24 hour emergency availability. All
vaccinations; pre- and post-travel
evaluation and consultation; treatment and lab testing on site.*

Hofstetter, Mark, MD
Pittsburgh Infectious Diseases, Ltd.
1400 Locust St.
Pittsburgh, PA 15219
412-232-7398

*Hours: 24. No limitation of practice.
Immunizations; complete lab.*

Rhode Island

Olds, G. Richard, MD
Associate: Peter M. Wiest, MD
Travelers' Clinics of the Interna-
    tional Health Institute, Brown
    University, Miriam Hospital
    Health Centers, Model C
164 Summit Ave.
Providence, RI 02906
401-274-3700 ext. 4075

*Hours: Wed. 8:30 a.m.-noon,
Fri. 8:30 a.m.-5 p.m. Telephone consultation available 40 hours/wk;
emergency consultation available 24
hours; all immunizations; various
medications and nonpharmaceuticals
related to foreign travel.*

South Carolina

Lettau, Ludwig A., MD, MPH
Department of Internal Medi
    cine/Infectious Diseases
Greenville Memorial Medical Ctr.
701 Grove Rd.
Greenville, SC 29605
803-242-7889

*Hours: Mon.-Fri. 9 a.m.-4:30 p.m.
Infectious diseases; tropical parasitic diseases; travel medicine;
immunizations.*

Tennessee

Schaffner, William, MD
Vanderbilt University Hospital
21st Ave. South
Nashville, TN 37232
615-322-2017

*Primarily consultation to hospital
patients; can arrange outpatient
evaluation, immunization.*

Texas

Price, T. M., MD
International Medicine Ctr.
7737 SW Freeway, #840
Houston, TX 77074
713-777-4547; Fax: 713-771-9007

Hours: 9 a.m.- 6 p.m. All vaccines.

Virginia

Guerrant, Richard L., MD, Head;
University of Virginia Travelers
  Clinic
University of Virginia Hospital
Department of Medicine - Box 485
Charlottesville, VA 22908
804-924-9677
Emergencies: 804-924-0000

*Hours: Wed. 1-4 p.m. Pre-travel pro-
phylaxis; evaluation and care of returning travelers.*

Washington

Jong, Elaine C., MD
Division of Infectious Diseases
UW Travel and Tropical Medicine
  Clinic
University of Washington School of
  Medicine
University Hospital RC-02
1959 NE Pacific
Seattle, WA 98195
206-548-4888 (and 206-548-4000,
206-548-4226)

*Hours: 24 hours. Routine and travel
immunizations; diagnosis and treatment of parasitic and tropical diseases.*

Karpilow, Craig, MD
Travelers Medical & Immunization
  Clinic of Seattle
509 Olive Way, Ste. 803
Seattle, WA 98101
206-624-6933 (24 hours)

*Hours: Mon.-Sat. by appointment.
Pre- and post-travel counseling; all
immunizations; on site lab; x-ray,
work with individuals or groups;
special health services for traveling
employees and executive travelers;
worldwide on-site consultations in
international occupational medicine;
treatment of tropical and other related diseases.*

West Virginia

Walden, John Beaumont, MD
Marshall University School of
  Medicine
1801 Sixth Ave.
Huntington, WV 25701
304-696-7046

*Hours: Mon.-Fri. 8 a.m.-5 p.m.
Traveler's advisory and clinical care
for tropical and parasitic diseases; all
immunizations.*

Travel notes

Index